THE
NATION'S

FAVOURITE
FOOD

The Nation's Favourite Food

Neven Maguire

GILL BOOKS

Gill Books
Hume Avenue
Park West
Dublin 12
www.gillbooks.ie

Gill Books is an imprint of M.H. Gill & Co.

© Neven Maguire 2013

978 07171 58553

Compiled by Orla Broderick
Edited by Kristin Jensen
Food styling by Sharon Hearne-Smith
Design by www.grahamthew.com
Photography © Joanne Murphy
Indexed by Eileen O'Neill
Printed in India by Replika Press Pvt. Ltd.

This book is typeset in 11 on 14pt Gibson Light.

The paper used in this book comes from the wood
pulp of managed forests. For every tree felled,
at least one tree is planted, thereby renewing
natural resources.

A CIP catalogue record for this book is available from
the British Library.

Props
Meadows & Byrne: Dublin, Cork, Galway,
Clare, Tipperary
t: 01 280 5444/021 434 4100
e: info@meadowsandbyrne.com
w: www.meadowsandbyrne.com

Arnotts, 12 Henry St, Dublin 1
t: 01 805 0400
e: customerservice@arnotts.ie
w: www.arnotts.ie

Dunnes Stores, nationwide
t: 01 475 1111
e: service.customer@dunnes-stores.ie
w: www.dunnesstores.ie

Stock Design, 33–34 South King Street, Dublin 2
t: 01 679 4317
e: stockdesign@eircom.net

Dedication

This book is dedicated to my wonderful wife, Amelda, who has been a great inspiration and support to me, and to the future generation, my twins Connor and Lucia, who have enjoyed and I hope will keep enjoying the food in this book.

Acknowledgements

It takes many people to make a great book, and this book simply could not have happened without my long-term collaborator, Orla Broderick. She is so knowledgeable and passionate about food, and has always been a great friend and support to me. She is a joy to work with and has made an enormous contribution to this book.

Sharon Hearne-Smith is a talented food stylist and, apart from this book, she also works on my television shows. I am always thrilled with the results. Thanks to Olivia Rafferty, Susan Murphy, Ajda Mehmet, Jette Virdi, Moya O'Dwyer and Lorna Ni Cheallaigh, who performed the crucial testing – and tasting! – of the recipes.

To Zara McHugh for deciphering my 'interesting' writing and typing all of the recipes. She did so much work with this book. Thank you, Zara.

Thanks also to Joanne Murphy for her lovely photography and Graham Thew for his design. The Gill & Macmillan team were a pleasure to work with again. A special thanks to Nicki Howard for such an inspirational idea for a book. Thanks to Catherine Gough, Kristin Jensen and Teresa Daly for all their work, and thank you to Michael Gill for his personal interest. They have given me another wonderful book.

RTÉ has played a huge part in my career. It began when John Masterson, my agent, believed in me and gave me my first break on *Open House* in 1998 – I can't thank him enough for that and for his friendship and support. Thank you to Purcell Masterson for advice and support over the years and thanks particularly to Mary Tallent, who is the best publicist I could ask for. Thank you also to my many friends in the media who have been so supportive.

David Hare has produced my television shows and has always been a pleasure to work with, along with cameraman, Billy Keady, and Ray de Brún on sound. Thank you also to Brian Walsh in RTÉ who has asked us back each year and has trusted us to deliver in prime time.

The *Irish Farmers Journal* has always been a great friend to me. Thank you to Mairead Lavery, David Leydon, and all the team – I enjoy my weekly column with you. And from day one Bord Bia have given me invaluable help.

I love heading to Dublin on a Saturday morning to chat with the one and only Marian Finucane. Thank you to Marian and to Anne Farrell for the opportunity. Another thank you to Bairbre Power and the *Irish Independent Weekend Magazine* for their continued support. It is great to work with my old *Open House*-mate Marty Whelan on Lyric FM. A special thank you to him. Thank you also to Sinead Wylde and all the Lyric team, who keep Marty on track!

Thank you to Eoin O'Flynn at Flogas for his continued support and friendship, and to Kenneth Maguire, my brother, and Andrea Doherty for organising all my demos and making sure things run smoothly.

Finally, thank you to all my supporters and the people I meet at the demos I do all over the country. You provide such great inspiration for my recipes and I hope you will enjoy many hours cooking the food in this book. Have fun!

Neven

Contents

Beef

Chicken

Lamb

Vegetarian

Takeaway My Way

Pasta

Dinner Party

Vegetable Sides

Lunchbox

Kids' Favourites

Desserts

Baking

Bread

Christmas

Basics

Index

Introduction

I have been cooking since I was the age of 12. I have been fortunate to learn from my mother, to train abroad, to try new flavours and new influences, and to keep working on my skills as a chef. I absolutely love and enjoy what I do.

I also love that I get to travel the length and breadth of the country every week doing cookery demonstrations and meeting people who enjoy cooking and want to better themselves. Every year I do hundreds of cookery demonstrations, from Belfast in the north to Wexford in the south, from Galway in the west to Dublin in the east. I meet thousands of people from all walks of life with all levels of skill in the kitchen. I meet people who have been cooking for years, mothers who put food on the table day after day and men who want to learn the latest technique. I also meet plenty of novice cooks who simply want to learn where to begin in the kitchen.

However, regardless of the person's level of skill or experience in the kitchen, I am repeatedly asked for the same things. What is my recipe for the perfect brown bread? Or my definitive method for the Christmas turkey? Or my failsafe recipe for chocolate cake, or mushroom soup, or the perfect steak?

And so here are my top 100 all-stars. The most requested recipes, the classics, the definitive versions of the food that we make and enjoy in Ireland every day.

We all experiment. Many of us try to get better and achieve restaurant-standard cooking with our foam and our jus, and yet we always come home to the classics. I know I do when I'm at home. After a day of demos or cooking in the restaurant, I want simple, tasty food. I know what it's like to cook for a hungry child, or a tired wife, or for entertaining friends and family, when you actually want to enjoy your guests rather than spend the evening in the kitchen. What you want is food that you know will work and be enjoyed, that always turns out as you'd hoped. I hope the recipes in this book will do that for you.

So I've taken these 100 recipes and refined them. Tested them. Tasted them. Added something. Taken something out. Freshened them up. Brought in new influences. Referred back to cookery bibles. Until I'm certain that they're as close to perfect as they can be. Until I can say to you that this is the definitive collection.

What do the people of Ireland make every day? You might be surprised. You will find bacon and cabbage and vegetable soup for sure, but you will also find chicken tikka masala and granola bars for life on the go.

I hope this book will be splattered with sauce, will have notes in the margins, will have the pages folded down. In short, I hope it becomes your trusted friend in the kitchen that you turn to time after time.

Most of all, I hope that you enjoy good food shared with your family and friends.

Neven Maguire

June 2013

SOUPS

Vera's Seafood Chowder

This recipe from my mum has been on and off the restaurant menu for as long as I can remember. It's actually very filling and more like a stew than a soup. Use the very best-quality fish and shellfish for the best flavour. **Serves 6**

1 tbsp rapeseed oil
15g (½ oz) butter, softened
2 celery sticks, cut into 1cm (½in) dice
1 small onion, cut into 1cm (½in) dice
1 carrot, cut into 1cm (½in) dice
1 large potato, cut into 1cm (½in) dice
½ small leek, cut into 1cm (½in) dice
1 tbsp plain flour
150ml (¼ pint) dry white wine
300ml (½ pint) fish stock (page 226)
100g (4oz) skinless salmon fillet, cut into
  cubes

100g (4oz) natural smoked haddock or
  cod fillet, cut into cubes
100g (4oz) cooked mussel meat
100g (4oz) cooked peeled prawns
150ml (¼ pint) cream
1 tsp chopped fresh flat-leaf parsley
1 tsp chopped fresh dill
sea salt and freshly ground black pepper
MacNean wheaten bread (page 203),
  to serve

Heat the oil in a large pan over a medium heat and then add the butter. Once it stops sizzling, tip in the celery, onion, carrot, potato and leek and cook for 5 minutes, or until softened but not coloured. Add the flour and cook on a low heat for 2 minutes, stirring continuously. Season to taste.

Gradually pour the wine into the pan and allow it to bubble down, stirring continuously, then add the stock and bring to the boil. Reduce the heat and simmer for 5 minutes. Stir in the salmon and smoked haddock or cod and simmer for 5 minutes, then add the mussel meat, prawns and cream and simmer for another 2–3 minutes, until warmed through. Stir in the herbs and season to taste.

To serve, ladle the soup into warmed bowls and serve with the wheaten bread.

Vegetable Soup with Barley

To me, this soup is the closest thing you'll get to a hug in a bowl. It's my mother's recipe and something she always made for me when I was little. I now make it for Amelda when she's feeling under the weather. Serves 4–6

50g (2oz) pearl barley
1 tbsp rapeseed oil
2 celery sticks, diced
1 onion, diced
1 carrot, diced
1 small leek, trimmed and diced
1 tsp chopped fresh thyme
50g (2oz) rindless streaky bacon, diced (optional)
1.2 litres (2 pints) vegetable or chicken stock (page 225 or 226)
1 tbsp chopped fresh flat-leaf parsley
sea salt and freshly ground black pepper
crusty bread, to serve (optional)

Place the pearl barley in a sieve and rinse well under cold running water.

Heat the rapeseed oil in a large pan over a medium heat and stir in the celery, onion, carrot, leek and thyme. Add the bacon, if using, and sauté for 5 minutes, until the vegetables are softened and the bacon is sizzling.

Pour in the stock, add the rinsed barley and bring to the boil, then reduce the heat and simmer for about 20 minutes, until the vegetables and barley are completely tender but still holding their shape. Stir in the parsley and season to taste.

To serve, ladle the soup into warmed bowls and have a separate basket of crusty bread, if liked.

Roasted Tomato and Pepper Soup

This is a great soup to make when you have a glut of tomatoes or ones that are slightly past their best. Like many of the soups that we now serve in the restaurant, it uses no flour to thicken it, so it's suitable for coeliacs. It's excellent hot or cold and I often put it on the vegetarian menu. **Serves 4–6**

1kg (2 ¼lb) vine-ripened tomatoes, halved
2 red peppers, quartered and seeds removed
2 tbsp rapeseed oil
1 tsp balsamic vinegar
½ tsp chopped fresh thyme
2 garlic cloves, crushed
1 large onion, finely chopped
900ml (1 ½ pints) vegetable or chicken stock (page 225 or 226)

4–6 tsp basil pesto (page 228)
handful of fresh basil leaves, to garnish

Croque monsieur:
4 slices white bread
4 slices cooked ham
75g (3oz) Cheddar cheese, grated
25g (1oz) butter, softened
sea salt and freshly ground black pepper

Preheat the oven to 190°C (375°F/gas mark 5).

Arrange the tomatoes and peppers in a baking tin, cut side up. Drizzle over 1 tablespoon of rapeseed oil and then sprinkle the vinegar and thyme on top. Place in the oven and roast for 20–25 minutes, until softened and lightly charred.

Heat the remaining tablespoon of oil in a large pan over a medium heat. Add the garlic and onion and sweat for 10 minutes, until lightly golden, stirring occasionally. Add the roasted tomatoes and peppers and the stock and bring to the boil. Reduce the heat and simmer for 10–15 minutes, until slightly reduced, then blitz with a hand blender until smooth. Season lightly and pass through a sieve for a really smooth finish.

When ready to serve, return the smooth soup to a clean pan and reheat it gently, stirring occasionally. Do not allow it to boil for too long or it will lose some of its wonderful vibrant colour.

Meanwhile, make the croque monsieur. Heat a large non-stick frying pan over a medium heat. Make 2 sandwiches with the bread, ham and cheese and then spread the butter on the outsides of the bread. Add the sandwiches to the heated frying pan and cook for 1–2 minutes on each side, until golden brown. Cut each sandwich into 4 fingers.

To serve, ladle the soup into warmed bowls and swirl a teaspoon of the basil pesto into each bowl. Scatter over the basil leaves and add a good grinding of black pepper. Put the bowls on plates and arrange the croque monsieur fingers on the side of each one.

French Onion Soup

If you have heatproof serving bowls, fill them with the piping hot soup and float the cheese croûtes on top and then grill until the cheese is bubbling and melted. I've used Gruyère cheese, which is traditional, but really any Irish cheese would work well, even Cheddar, or use a mixture of both. Serves 4–6

50g (2oz) butter
675g (1 ½lb) onions, thinly sliced
1 tbsp caster sugar
25g (1oz) plain flour
1 litre (1 ¾ pints) beef stock (page 227)
1 tbsp cider vinegar

Gruyère croûtes:
8–12 thin slices baguette
100g (4oz) Gruyère cheese, grated
50g (2oz) crème fraîche
1 tsp snipped fresh chives, extra to garnish
sea salt and freshly ground black pepper

Melt the butter in a large pan and add the onions and sugar. Cook the onions over a very low heat for 40–50 minutes, until well softened and golden brown, stirring occasionally so that the onions don't stick as they caramelise.

Stir the flour into the onions and cook over a very low heat for another 5 minutes, stirring continuously. Gradually pour in the stock and add the vinegar, stirring to prevent any lumps from forming. Bring to the boil, then reduce the heat and simmer for 15–20 minutes, until the onions are meltingly tender and the soup has thickened, stirring occasionally. Season to taste.

Preheat the grill to high. Arrange the baguette slices on the grill rack and toast on both sides. Mix the Gruyère with the crème fraîche and chives. Season to taste and spread over the slices of toasted baguette. Place under the grill for another 1–2 minutes, until the cheese is bubbling and melted.

To serve, ladle the soup into warmed bowls and arrange the bubbling Gruyère croûtes on top. Sprinkle over the chives to serve.

Wild Mushroom Soup

Mushroom soup made from wild mushrooms has the most extraordinary, intense flavour. I find they actually make the best soup when they are a few days old and have darkened a bit, so snatch up any that are just past their best in the supermarket. If you want a gluten-free soup, omit the bread and reduce the stock. Serves 6

25g (1oz) dried cep mushrooms
50g (2oz) butter
1 onion, finely chopped
1 garlic clove, crushed
450g (1lb) wild mushrooms (such as chantarelle, shiitake and oyster), sliced
1.2 litres (2 pints) vegetable or chicken stock (page 225 or 226)
75g (3oz) sourdough bread, crusts removed

150ml (¼ pint) cream, extra to garnish
1 tsp snipped fresh chives

Parmesan croutons:
175g (6oz) sourdough bread
1 garlic clove, crushed
25g (1oz) freshly grated Parmesan
1 tbsp olive oil
sea salt and freshly ground black pepper

Preheat the oven to 180°C (350°F/gas mark 4).

To make the croutons, cut the crusts off the bread and cut the bread into small cubes. Place in a bowl with the garlic, Parmesan and oil. Season to taste and mix well to combine. Tip out onto a baking dish and cook for 10–12 minutes, tossing once or twice to ensure the croutons cook evenly, until golden brown and crunchy. Set aside until needed.

To make the soup, soak the dried ceps in 150ml (¼ pint) of boiling water for 15 minutes. Drain and reserve the soaking liquid. Finely chop the reconstituted mushrooms and set aside.

Melt half of the butter in a large pan over a medium heat and gently cook the onion and garlic for 10 minutes, until softened but not coloured. Increase the heat, add the wild mushrooms and stir-fry for 3–4 minutes, until just tender. Pour in the stock and reserved mushroom soaking liquid and add the reconstituted ceps. Bring to the boil, then reduce the heat and simmer for 15–20 minutes, until the mushrooms are tender and the liquid has slightly reduced.

Crumble the bread into the soup, then purée in batches in a food processor or with a hand-held blender. Pour the soup back into the pan, season to taste and add the cream. Reheat gently but do not let it boil.

To serve, ladle the soup into warmed bowls and garnish each one with a drizzle of cream, the chives and the Parmesan croutons.

STARTERS

Mixed Fish Platter with Pickled Cucumber and Red Onion

A lovely, easy starter with gorgeous flavours that's just down to some clever shopping.
Much of it can be made ahead of time, leaving you to enjoy your guests. Serves 4–6

Pickled cucumber and red onion:
4 tbsp rice wine vinegar
2 tbsp caster sugar
1 baby cucumber, pared into thin strips
    with a vegetable peeler and then
    halved lengthways
1 red onion, cut into fine wedges

Smoked mackerel pâté:
225g (8oz) smoked mackerel fillets
73g (3oz) cream cheese
1 tbsp snipped fresh chives, extra to
    garnish
1 tbsp creamed horseradish
1 tsp prepared English mustard
juice of ½ lemon
dash of Tabasco

Garlic stuffed mussels:
450g (1lb) fresh mussels
50g (2oz) butter
2 garlic cloves, crushed
50g (2oz) fresh white breadcrumbs
1 tbsp chopped fresh flat-leaf parsley
squeeze of fresh lemon juice

Sizzling seafood:
4 tbsp olive oil
knob of butter
1 red chilli, halved, seeded and cut into
    rings
1 garlic clove, thinly sliced
12 large raw Dublin Bay prawns, peeled
    and cleaned
12 crab claws
½ lemon, pips removed
1 tbsp chopped fresh flat-leaf parsley
sea salt and freshly ground black pepper

To serve:
225g (8oz) slices organic smoked salmon
8–12 slices MacNean wheaten bread
    (page 203)
lemon wedges, to garnish

To make the pickled cucumber and red onion, place the vinegar in a serving bowl and stir in
the sugar to dissolve. Add the cucumber strips and onion wedges and toss to coat. Cover with
clingfilm and set aside for at least 10 minutes, or up to 8 hours in the fridge is fine.

To make the mackerel pâté, remove the skin from the mackerel fillets and discard any bones,
then break up the flesh into a bowl. Add the cream cheese, chives, horseradish, mustard, lemon

juice and Tabasco. Mix thoroughly until well combined and season to taste, then transfer to a serving bowl. Chill until needed.

To make the garlic stuffed mussels, first tap any opened mussels on the counter and discard any that don't close. Place the mussels in a shallow, heavy-based pan. Cover with a tight-fitting lid and cook over a high heat for 3–5 minutes, shaking occasionally, until all the mussels have opened (discard any that don't). Remove the top shell from each mussel and arrange the bottom shell and flesh in a shallow ovenproof dish. Melt the butter in a small pan. Stir in the garlic, breadcrumbs, parsley and lemon juice. Place a little of the mixture onto each of the mussels. When ready to serve, place them under a medium grill for 3–5 minutes, until the breadcrumbs are golden brown.

To make the sizzling seafood, heat the olive oil and the knob of butter in a large frying pan over a medium heat. Once the butter has stopped sizzling, add the chilli and garlic and sauté for about 30 seconds, until the garlic is lightly golden. Tip in the prepared prawns and sauté for another few minutes, until tender. When the prawns start to change in colour and begin to curl, tip in the crab claws and allow to warm through, but be careful not to overcook them. Add a good squeeze of lemon juice and sprinkle over the parsley, tossing to coat. Season to taste and tip into a warmed serving bowl.

To serve, garnish the mackerel pâté with chives and put on the table with the bowl of pickled cucumber and red onion, a dish of the garlic stuffed mussels and a bowl of the sizzling seafood. Arrange the smoked salmon and wheaten bread on a board and garnish with the lemon wedges.

Antipasti Platter with Crispy Flatbreads

This deliciously informal antipasti platter looks absolutely stunning when served like this. The whole thing can be prepared from start to finish in a matter of minutes – perfect for a summer supper or to serve as nibbles before a long, lazy Sunday lunch. Serves 4–6

Avocado hummus:
400g (14oz) can chickpeas, rinsed and drained
2 garlic cloves, crushed
1 ripe Hass avocado, halved, stoned and flesh scooped out
100ml (3 ½fl oz) light tahini (sesame seed paste) (optional)
juice of 1 lemon
4 tbsp water
2 tbsp extra virgin olive oil
good pinch of ground cumin
sea salt

Artichoke and feta dip:
285g (10oz) jar marinated artichoke hearts in oil, well drained
100g (4oz) feta cheese, roughly chopped
1 tbsp fresh lemon juice
3 tbsp extra virgin olive oil

Peppadews with goat's cheese:
150g (5oz) soft goat's cheese
½ jar Peppadew peppers, drained

Crispy flatbreads:
4–6 soft flour tortillas
olive oil, for brushing

To serve:
extra virgin olive oil, for dressing
good pinch of paprika
6 slices Parma ham
2 tsp snipped fresh chives
75g (3oz) sun-dried tomatoes, drained
75g (3oz) marinated black olives, drained
25g (1oz) wild rocket
½ tsp balsamic vinegar
sea salt and freshly ground black pepper

To make the avocado hummus, combine the chickpeas, garlic, avocado, tahini (if using), lemon juice, water, oil and cumin in a food processor and whizz to a creamy purée. Season with salt and turn out into a serving bowl, then smooth the top with the back of a spoon. Cover with clingfilm and chill until needed (this will keep in the fridge for a few hours).

To make the artichoke and feta dip, place the drained artichoke hearts in a food processor with the feta and lemon juice. Blitz to form a smooth paste, then with the motor running, slowly add the olive oil until well combined. Season to taste and spoon into a serving bowl. Cover with clingfilm and chill until needed.

To make the Peppadew peppers with goat's cheese, season the goat's cheese and use it to fill a disposable piping bag, then pipe into the Peppadews. Cover with clingfilm and chill until needed.

To prepare the crispy flatbreads, preheat the oven to 200°C (400°F/gas mark 6). Place 2 baking sheets in the oven for about 5 minutes, until well heated. Meanwhile, brush both sides of the soft flour tortillas with olive oil, then cut in half. Cut each half into four triangles and arrange on the heated baking sheets. Place in the oven for 3–4 minutes, until crisped up and light gold in colour.

To serve, drizzle a little extra virgin olive oil over the bowls of avocado hummus and the artichoke and feta dip. Add a little paprika to the avocado hummus and a little black pepper to the artichoke dip. Arrange the slices of Parma ham on a board with the crsipy flatbreads and nice loose mounds of the Peppadew peppers with goat's cheese sprinkled with the chives. Put the sun-dried tomatoes and olives in separate small serving bowls. Tip the rocket into a serving bowl and dress with extra virgin olive oil and the balsamic vinegar. Season to taste and put everything on the table so that your guests can help themselves.

Prawn Cocktail

Although prawn cocktail might seem a bit dated, it has enjoyed a resurgence in popularity in recent years. Made properly with fresh ingredients, it can make an elegant yet simple starter that no one will forget in a hurry. Serves 4

Marinated cherry tomatoes:
10 small cherry tomatoes, halved
1 tbsp extra virgin olive oil
dash of balsamic vinegar

Marie Rose sauce:
4 tbsp mayonnaise
2 tbsp tomato ketchup
1 tbsp extra virgin olive oil
½ tsp prepared English mustard
dash of Tabasco
dash of Worcestershire sauce
squeeze of lemon juice

Guacamole:
2 ripe Hass avocados
2 tbsp mayonnaise
juice of 1 lime

To serve:
20 small Little Gem lettuce leaves,
   trimmed
4 lemon wedges
20 large Dublin Bay prawns, cooked and
   peeled
small handful of fresh chives, cut into
   5cm (2in) pieces
sea salt and freshly ground black pepper

To make the marinated tomatoes, place the cherry tomatoes in a bowl and season generously. Sprinkle over the olive oil and balsamic vinegar. Cover with clingfilm and set aside at room temperature for at least 10 minutes (or up to 1 hour is fine) to allow the flavours to mingle.

To make the Marie Rose sauce, whisk together the mayonnaise, ketchup, olive oil, mustard, Tabasco and Worcestershire in a bowl. Season to taste and add a squeeze of lemon juice. Cover with clingfilm and chill until needed.

To make the guacamole, cut the avocados in half and remove the stones. Put the flesh in a bowl and mash to a purée. Stir in the mayonnaise and lime juice and season to taste. Cover with clingfilm and chill for up to 2 hours.

To serve, arrange 5 Little Gem lettuce leaves on each serving plate and put a lemon wedge in the middle of each plate. Add small spoonfuls of the guacamole, the cooked prawns, marinated cherry tomatoes and teaspoons of the Marie Rose sauce. Garnish each one with a piece of chive.

Bruschetta Platter

Bruschetta makes delicious, simple nibbles and can look very impressive when laid out on platters. Alternatively, use slices of French batons to make little bruschetta (crostini). Don't be tempted to make this too far in advance, as the bread goes soggy. Serves 6

Bruschetta:
about 24 slices country bread
1 garlic clove, halved
4 tbsp extra virgin olive oil
sea salt and freshly ground black pepper

Melted Brie with fig jam:
1 tbsp rapeseed oil
1 red onion, thinly sliced
100g (4oz) ready-to-eat figs, finely chopped
1 garlic clove, crushed
75ml (3fl oz) red wine
1 tbsp balsamic vinegar
½ tsp caster sugar
½ tsp chopped fresh thyme
175g (6oz) ripe Brie, cut into thin slices

Air-dried beef with beetroot and horseradish:
50g (2oz) crème fraîche
1 tbsp creamed horseradish
2 tsp wholegrain mustard
6 slices air-dried beef, cut in half (at room temperature)
6 tbsp beetroot relish (from a jar)
25g (1oz) fresh small watercress sprigs
25g (1oz) walnut halves, toasted
15g (½oz) Parmesan shavings

Parma ham and rocket rolls:
75g (3oz) ricotta cheese
1 tbsp basil pesto (page 228 or shop-bought)
8 slices Parma ham
25g (1oz) wild rocket, tough stalks removed

To prepare the bruschetta, preheat the grill or a griddle pan and use it to toast the bread on both sides. Remove from the heat and immediately rub one side with a piece of garlic, then drizzle over the olive oil.

To make the fig jam for the Brie topping, heat the oil in a pan over a medium heat and sauté the red onion for 10 minutes, until softened. Stir in the figs, garlic, red wine and balsamic vinegar. Simmer for about 10 minutes, until most of the liquid has evaporated, then stir in the sugar and thyme. Season to taste, then blend until smooth and leave to cool. When ready to serve, spread the fig jam over 10 of the bruschetta and cover with the Brie. Place under a medium grill for a minute or so, until it's just beginning to melt. Season with pepper.

To make the mustard cream for the air-dried beef topping, place the crème fraîche, horseradish and mustard in a bowl and mix well to combine, then season to taste. When ready to serve, spread a little mustard cream on 6 pieces of the bruschetta and arrange the air-dried beef on top. Add a spoonful of the beetroot relish and garnish with the watercress sprigs, the rest of the mustard cream, walnuts and Parmesan. Finish with a sprinkling of pepper.

To make the Parma ham and rocket topping, mix the ricotta cheese with the pesto in a bowl and season generously. Cut each slice of Parma ham in half across the width and arrange on a work surface. Spread a heaped teaspoon of the ricotta mixture in a thin, even layer over each piece of Parma ham and then lay a few sprigs of rocket lengthways across each slice, leaving the sprig ends poking out of the top. Roll up each one to enclose.

Arrange the Parma ham and rocket rolls on 8 of the bruschetta and put on a large platter with the melted Brie and fig jam bruschetta and the air-dried beef bruschetta.

Chicken Liver Pâté with Onion Jam

I know how easy it is to buy pâté these days, but nothing tastes as good as homemade. This recipe can be prepared ahead and will keep for 3 to 4 days in the fridge. I love the contrast between the sweet onion jam and the savoury pâté. Serves 6

400g (14oz) fresh chicken livers, trimmed
300ml (½ pint) milk
225g (8oz) unsalted butter
3 shallots, finely chopped
1 garlic clove, crushed
½ tsp chopped fresh thyme
1 tbsp port
1 tbsp Madeira
4 eggs
1 tbsp cream
toast triangles, to serve
lightly dressed salad leaves, to serve

Onion jam:
25g (1oz) butter
2 red onions, thinly sliced
50g (2oz) light muscovado sugar
75ml (3fl oz) red wine
3 tbsp balsamic vinegar
1 tbsp dark soy sauce
sea salt and freshly ground black pepper

To make the pâté, soak the chicken livers in a bowl with the milk overnight in the fridge. The next day, drain off the milk and rinse the livers under cold running water, then dry thoroughly with kitchen paper.

Heat a frying pan over a medium heat and add 25g (1oz) of the butter. Tip in the shallots, garlic and thyme and cook for a couple of minutes, until softened. Pour over the port and Madeira and cook for another minute to burn off the alcohol. Remove from the heat and leave to cool. Melt 75g (3oz) of the butter and set aside to cool a little.

Preheat the oven to 160°C (325°F/gas mark 3). Line a 450g (1lb) loaf tin with clingfilm (or you could use a Pyrex dish).

Purée the chicken livers in a food processor for about 3 minutes, until well blended. Add the shallot mixture and blend again for 30 seconds. Add the eggs, cream and melted butter through the feeder tube. Blend again briefly and then season generously.

Pass the chicken liver mixture through a sieve and pour into the lined loaf tin or Pyrex dish. Cover tightly with tin foil and place in a roasting tin half filled with hot water (otherwise known as a bain marie). Place in the oven for about 1 hour, or until the pâté is set. Leave to cool and then put in the fridge for 1–2 hours to chill down, or overnight is best.

Melt the remaining 100g (4oz) butter in a small pan and then pour it into a jug. Leave to cool a little and settle. Pour a layer over the set chicken liver pâté, leaving behind any milky white sediment. This will preserve the pâté.

To make the onion jam, melt the butter in a heavy-based pan. Add the red onions, sugar, red wine, vinegar and soy sauce. Sauté for 5 minutes over a medium heat, tossing occasionally. Sprinkle over 1 tablespoon of water, then reduce the temperature and cook gently for 25–30 minutes. The onions should make a soft, sticky, sweet and sour jam. Season to taste and leave to cool. Transfer to a bowl, then cover with clingfilm and chill until needed.

To serve, carefully remove the layer of butter that has preserved the pâté and then scoop out spoonfuls or cut into slices and arrange on plates with the onion jam, toast triangles and salad leaves.

SALADS

Broccoli, Feta and Cherry Tomato Salad

I just love this simple salad, with its variety of textures and flavours. The broccoli can be left raw if you prefer, but I like to blanch it long enough to bring up its colour. If you want to prepare it in advance, just leave out the hazelnuts until the last minute or they may lose their crunch.
Serves 4–6

450g (1lb) head of broccoli, broken into small florets
225g (8oz) cherry tomatoes, halved
175g (6oz) feta cheese
handful of roasted, skinned hazelnuts, roughly chopped

Mustard dressing:
1 tbsp white wine vinegar
pinch of caster sugar
pinch of salt
4 tbsp extra virgin olive oil
1 tbsp snipped fresh chives
1 tsp Dijon mustard
1 tsp wholegrain mustard
sea salt and freshly ground black pepper

To make the mustard dressing, place the vinegar in a screw-topped jar and add the sugar and a good pinch of salt, then shake until the salt has dissolved. Add the oil to the jar with the chives and mustards and shake again until you have formed a thick emulsion. Season to taste and chill until needed.

Blanch the broccoli for 1–2 minutes in a pan of boiling salted water, then drain and quickly refresh under cold running water. Tip into a serving bowl and scatter over the cherry tomatoes. Using your hands, break up the feta cheese into small pieces and sprinkle on top.

To serve, drizzle the mustard dressing over the broccoli, cherry tomatoes and feta and then add the hazelnuts. Gently fold in until well combined.

Bellingham Blue and Fennel Salad with Watercress, Pears and Walnuts

Bellingham Blue is a creamy, blue-veined, award-winning Irish cheese that is handmade by Peter and Anita Thomas in Louth from a herd of Friesian cows. As an unpasteurised cheese it has a distinct tangy, almost nutty flavour with a slight hint of fruit. Serves 4

3 tbsp extra virgin olive oil
1 tbsp white wine vinegar
1 tsp Dijon mustard
1 small fennel bulb, with fronds intact
50g (2oz) fresh watercress sprigs, well picked over
1 firm, ripe pear, cored and thinly sliced
200g (7oz) Bellingham Blue, roughly crumbled
25g (1oz) toasted walnut halves or pieces, roughly chopped
sea salt and freshly ground black pepper

To make the dressing, whisk the olive oil, vinegar and mustard in a small bowl, adding a little water if the dressing becomes too thick. Season to taste.

Using a Japanese mandolin, thinly slice the fennel and toss it in half of the dressing. Reserve the fronds to garnish.

To serve, arrange the dressed fennel on a platter and scatter over the watercress, pear slices, Bellingham Blue and walnuts. Drizzle the rest of the dressing on top and garnish with the reserved fennel fronds.

Beetroot Carpaccio with Walnut Pesto and Goat's Cheese

To make your own balsamic syrup, bring the contents of a bottle of balsamic vinegar to the boil and simmer until reduced by half to a honey consistency, then leave to cool. We store ours in small squeezy bottles for convenience. I love to use it because it intensifies the flavour of the vinegar, making it thick and syrupy, and it looks great when drizzled onto a plate. Serves 4

1 large raw beetroot
450ml (¾ pint) red wine
100ml (3 ½fl oz) ruby red port
2 tbsp Demerara sugar
500g (1lb 2oz) soft goat's cheese, at room temperature
2 tsp snipped fresh chives
1 punnet salad cress
4 tsp balsamic syrup (page 229)

Walnut pesto:
100g (4oz) toasted walnut halves or pieces, finely chopped
1 small Granny Smith apple, cored and finely diced
small handful of fresh basil leaves, finely chopped
100ml (3 ½fl oz) rapeseed oil
sea salt and freshly ground black pepper

To prepare the beetroot, it's best to put a pair of gloves on, otherwise you will stain your hands. Trim the top off the beetroot and then peel. Using a mandolin, carefully slice the beetroot as thinly as possible. You'll need 24 even-sized slices for this recipe in total.

Place the wine in a pan with the port and Demerara sugar. Bring to the boil, then reduce to a simmer and add the thinly sliced beetroot and cook for 15–20 minutes, or until just cooked through. Drain well and dry with kitchen paper.

Meanwhile, make the walnut pesto. Place the walnuts in a bowl with the apple, basil and oil. Season to taste and stir until well combined.

Place the goat's cheese in a bowl and stir until soft. Stir in the chives and season to taste. Spoon into a piping bag with a 2.5cm (1in) plain nozzle.

To serve, arrange 3 slices of beetroot on each serving plate and pipe the goat's cheese on top, then drizzle over a little of the walnut pesto. Cover each one with another slice of beetroot. Cut the salad cress with a scissors and scatter on top, then spoon over the remaining walnut pesto and add dots of the balsamic syrup.

Caesar Salad

There are those who hesitate when it comes to using anchovies in a Caesar salad, but they are vital. Don't worry about marinated anchovies, as a well-made Caesar salad doesn't need unnecessary adornment. Traditionally the dressing would be made with a one-minute coddled or boiled egg yolk, but perhaps life is too short to be that precise. Serves 4–6

2 large Cos lettuces or 6 Little Gem
  lettuces, separated into leaves
75g (3oz) freshly grated Parmesan, extra
  to garnish

Parmesan croutons:
175g (6oz) country-style bread, crusts
  removed, and cut into 1cm (½in) cubes
3 tbsp olive oil
25g (1oz) freshly grated Parmesan

Dressing:
50g (2oz) can anchovy fillets, drained
1 garlic clove, crushed
1 egg yolk
2 tsp red wine vinegar
2 tsp lemon juice
2 tsp Dijon mustard
1 tsp Worcestershire sauce
¼ tsp dry English mustard powder
150ml (¼ pint) light olive oil
sea salt and freshly ground black pepper

Preheat the oven to 150°C (300°F/gas mark 2).

To make the Parmesan croutons, place the bread cubes in a baking dish and drizzle over the olive oil, then season generously. Toss until well combined and bake for 20 minutes, then remove from the oven and scatter over the Parmesan. Return to the oven and bake for another 20–25 minutes, until crisp and golden brown, stirring occasionally. These can be made in advance and stored in an airtight container.

To make the dressing, mash 3 of the anchovy fillets to a paste and place in a food processor with the garlic, egg yolk, vinegar, lemon juice, Dijon mustard, Worcestershire sauce, mustard powder and black pepper to taste (½ to 1 teaspoon is about right). Blend together until well combined. With the machine running, pour in the oil in a slow trickle through the feeder tube.

To serve, tear the lettuce leaves into bite-sized pieces and place in a large bowl. Add enough of the dressing to just coat (not drown) the leaves, then fold in the Parmesan. Toss to combine, then transfer to wide-rimmed serving bowls, scatter over the Parmesan croutons and add the remaining anchovies. Garnish with the extra freshly grated Parmesan.

Puy Lentil, Red Onion and Sun-dried Tomato Salad

Puy lentils have a greeny, slate-grey colour and definitely the best flavour. If your local super-market doesn't have any, you should have more luck in a health food shop. Or if you're in a hurry, used canned Puy lentils, which require no cooking. I like to make this salad a little while before I need it so that all the flavours have time to soak into the lentils. Serves 4

225g (8oz) Puy lentils, washed
2 garlic cloves, peeled
1 bay leaf
1 tsp red wine vinegar
pinch of caster sugar
1 large red onion, finely chopped
50g (2oz) sun-dried tomatoes in oil, drained and chopped
6 tbsp coarsely chopped fresh flat-leaf parsley
4 tbsp extra virgin olive oil
1 tbsp balsamic vinegar
175g (6oz) goat's cheese or feta cheese, crumbled
sea salt and freshly ground black pepper
crusty bread, to serve (optional)

Place the lentils in a pan with 1 garlic clove, the bay leaf, vinegar and the sugar. Season to taste and cover with 1.2 litres (2 pints) of cold water. Bring to the boil, then reduce the heat and simmer for 25 minutes, or until the lentils are just tender but still holding their shape.

Drain the lentils well, discarding the whole garlic clove and the bay leaf. Tip into a bowl and leave to cool completely.

Finely chop the remaining garlic clove and stir it into the lentils with the red onion, sun-dried tomatoes, parsley, extra virgin olive oil and balsamic vinegar. Season to taste and stir well to combine, then carefully fold in the goat's cheese or feta. Cover with clingfilm and set aside at room temperature to allow the flavours to develop.

To serve, divide the salad among serving plates and eat with some crusty bread, if liked.

The Ultimate Beef Burger with Crispy Potato Wedges

A really good burger has to be made from really good beef. If you can, ask a butcher to mince some rump, blade or chuck steak for you, but make sure it has 20 per cent fat content, as in effect this will make them self-basting and will prevent them from drying out during cooking. Otherwise, buy ordinary minced beef from the supermarket, but don't buy extra-lean mince or the burgers will become tough during cooking. **Serves 4**

675g (1 ½lb) minced beef (see the intro)
1 small onion, finely grated
1 mild red chilli, seeded and finely chopped (optional)
1 garlic clove, crushed
2 tbsp cream
1 tbsp chopped fresh flat-leaf parsley
½ heaped tsp salt
freshly ground black pepper
4 slices Cheddar
2 tbsp mayonnaise
50g (2oz) iceberg lettuce, finely shredded
25g (1oz) cocktail gherkins, finely chopped
2 tbsp finely chopped spring onion
1 tsp Dijon mustard
4 sesame bread rolls or baps, halved
2 tomatoes, thinly sliced
Ballymaloe tomato relish, to serve

Crispy potato wedges:
4 x 175g (6oz) potatoes, scrubbed (about 675g/1 ½lb in total)
2 tbsp olive oil
2 tsp Cajun seasoning
½ tsp salt
freshly ground black pepper

Place the minced beef in a food processor and add the onion, chilli (if using), garlic, double cream and parsley. Season with the salt and plenty of pepper, then quickly blitz until the meat starts to hold together. Divide the mixture into 4 burgers and shape by hand or by pressing into a metal pastry cutter. Arrange on a flat plate, then cover loosely with clingfilm and chill for at least 1 hour to allow the mixture to firm up.

To make the crispy potato wedges, preheat the oven to 200°C (400°F/gas mark 6). Cut each potato into 8 even-sized wedges. Place the potatoes in a pan of boiling water, return to the boil and blanch for 2–3 minutes, then quickly drain.

Put the olive oil in a large roasting tin with the Cajun seasoning, salt and some freshly ground black pepper. Add the wedges and toss until they are all well coated in the flavoured oil, then arrange them in rows 'sitting' upright on their skins. Bake for 35–40 minutes, until completely tender and lightly golden.

Meanwhile, preheat the grill or a barbecue with medium-hot coals and cook the burgers for about 5 minutes on each side for medium. Put a slice of Cheddar on top of each one and then remove from the heat. Leave to cool for a couple of minutes in a warm place until the cheese has just started to melt. Place the mayonnaise in a bowl and mix in the lettuce, gherkins, spring onion and mustard. Season to taste and mix well.

To serve, lightly toast the cut sides of the rolls under the grill or on the barbecue for 1–2 minutes. Cover the bottom half with a couple of slices of tomato and some lettuce mayonnaise, then sit the burger with the melting Cheddar on top. Cover with the top half of the bun and arrange on warmed serving plates with the crispy potato wedges and a small pot of tomato relish.

Beef Bourguignon

This all-time classic shows that a combination of beef and red Burgundy wine is a winner every time. It needs nothing more than a large basket of crusty bread. I think this only improves with time and I often make it a couple of days before I plan to serve it. Serves 4–6

25g (1oz) butter
2 tbsp sunflower oil
350g (12oz) small shallots, peeled
100g (4oz) pancetta or rindless streaky
  bacon
675g (1 ½lb) chuck steak, cut into
  bite-sized pieces
50g (2oz) seasoned flour
1 bottle red Burgundy wine
150ml (¼ pint) beef stock (page 227)

2 carrots, chopped
2 celery sticks, chopped
2 bay leaves
2 tsp fresh thyme leaves
225g (8oz) small chestnut mushrooms,
  trimmed
2 tbsp brandy
sea salt and freshly ground black pepper
crusty French bread, to serve

Heat half of the butter and 1 tablespoon of the oil in a large frying pan over a medium heat. Add the shallots and fry for 3–4 minutes, until they're just beginning to brown, then tip in the pancetta or bacon and fry until lightly browned. Transfer to a plate with a slotted spoon.

Place the beef pieces in a ziplock bag with the seasoned flour. Toss until the beef is well coated with the flour, then remove, shaking off any excess flour. Add to the frying pan and fry until lightly golden on all sides. Transfer to a casserole dish with a lid.

Add a little of the red wine to the frying pan and scrape the bottom to remove any sediment, then pour this in on top of the beef with the rest of the red wine and the stock, carrots, celery, bay leaves and thyme. Add the sautéed shallots and pancetta and season with salt and pepper. Stir to combine, then cover and simmer gently for 1 ½ hours, or until the meat is tender but still holding its shape.

Halfway through cooking, heat the remaining butter and 1 tablespoon of the oil in a large frying pan over a medium heat and cook the mushrooms for 3–4 minutes, until just tender and lightly browned, stirring. Add the brandy and cook for another few minutes, then stir into the casserole dish and return to the oven for the remaining cooking time.

When the beef bourguignon is ready, season to taste and serve straight to the table with a separate bowl of crusty French bread to hand around.

Roast Rib of Beef on the Bone with Crispy Roast Potatoes

A rib of beef is an excellent cut for roasting and perfect when you have to feed a crowd. Always allow a joint to come to room temperature before roasting to achieve the best flavour. The key to its success is to start with a fantastic piece of beef that has been hung for 21 days to improve the flavour and texture. Serves 4–6

1 tsp black peppercorns
1 tbsp English mustard powder
2 tsp sea salt flakes
1.5kg (3lb) French trimmed rib of
  beef on the bone, tied with string
2 tbsp olive oil
2 large onions, quartered with root intact
2 large carrots, halved lengthways
675g (1 ½lb) potatoes, halved or
  quartered

1 garlic bulb, broken into cloves
  (not peeled)
small handful soft thyme leaves
2 tsp plain flour
400ml (14fl oz) chicken or beef stock
  (page 226 or 227)
sea salt and freshly ground black pepper
creamed horseradish, to serve

Preheat the oven to 230°C (450°F/gas mark 8).

Heat a small frying pan and toast the peppercorns until aromatic, then place in a pestle and mortar and grind until cracked. Mix in the mustard and salt. Wipe the meat with damp kitchen paper and rub with the mustard mixture.

Pour the olive oil into a roasting tin and add the onions, carrots, potatoes, garlic and thyme, tossing to coat. Season to taste, then push the veg to the edges and sit the beef in the middle of the vegetables. Roast for 15 minutes and then reduce the oven temperature to 200°C (400°F/gas mark 6) and roast for 10 minutes per 450g (1lb) for rare, 12 minutes for medium-rare and 20–25 minutes for well done. Take out and baste halfway through the cooking time and quickly turn over the roast potatoes.

Remove the beef, onions and carrots from the tin and place on a platter. Cover with tin foil and leave to rest for 15 minutes before carving. Pop the potatoes and garlic into another roasting tin and continue to cook in the oven, removing the garlic cloves if they are starting to catch and burn.

To make the gravy, pour the juices from the roasting tin into a jug and leave the fat to settle on top, then skim off the fat and discard, reserving the juices. Stir the flour into the roasting tin, scraping the bottom of the tin with a wooden spoon to remove any residue, then gradually stir in the stock and reserved juices. Place the tin directly on the hob and simmer for 5 minutes, stirring. Pour through a sieve into a gravy boat.

To serve, carve the rested beef into slices and arrange on warmed serving plates with a dollop of creamed horseradish. Add the roasted onions, carrots and potatoes. Hand round the gravy separately.

Grilled Rib-eye Steak with Smoky Red Pepper Butter

I hear that less fillet and striploin is being sold these days and rib-eye has become more popular, as it's good value. I always bring steaks to room temperature by removing them from the fridge 30 minutes before I want to cook them. This butter or any of the variations on pages 42–43 will complement any grilled meat and it looks great. It can be frozen or it keeps happily in the fridge for up to 2 weeks. **Serves 4**

4 x 225g (8oz) dry-aged rib-eye steaks
100ml (3 ½fl oz) olive oil
2 garlic cloves, crushed
1 tsp chopped fresh thyme
sea salt and freshly ground black pepper
baked potatoes, to serve
steamed purple sprouting broccoli,
   to serve

Smoky red pepper butter:
1 small red pepper
100g (4oz) butter, softened
1 tsp chopped fresh flat-leaf parsley
1 tsp smoked paprika
½ tsp chopped fresh thyme
1 tbsp cream

To make the flavoured butter, preheat the grill. Place the pepper on the grill rack and cook for 20–25 minutes, until the skin is blackened and blistered. Transfer to a bowl and cover with clingfilm, then leave to cool completely.

Remove the skin, core and seeds from the pepper and roughly chop the flesh, then place in a food processor. Add the butter, parsley, paprika and thyme and purée until smooth. Beat in the cream and then scrape the butter out onto a square of parchment paper. Roll into a cylinder about 2.5cm (1in) thick, twisting the ends to secure. Chill for at least 2 hours to harden.

Trim the rib-eye steaks of any excess fat. Place in a non-metallic dish and add the olive oil, garlic and thyme. Cover with clingfilm and marinate in the fridge for at least 2 hours or overnight is best.

Remove the steaks from the fridge at least 30 minutes before you want to cook them, then shake off any excess marinade and season to taste. Grill, barbecue or pan-fry the steaks over a fierce heat for 6–7 minutes for medium rare, or to your liking. Allow to rest for 5 minutes on warmed serving plates.

To serve, remove the flavoured butter from the fridge and remove the paper, then cut the butter into slices. Place butter slices on top of the grilled steaks and add a baked potato and some purple sprouting broccoli to each plate to serve.

Variations

Blue Cheese and Celery Sauce
Makes 325ml (11fl oz)

1 tbsp olive oil
large knob of butter
2 celery sticks, thinly sliced
1 small onion, finely chopped
100ml (3 ½fl oz) port
100ml (3 ½fl oz) dry white wine
100ml (3 ½fl oz) beef stock (page 227)
100ml (3 ½fl oz) cream
100g (4oz) blue cheese (such as Cashel Blue), rind removed and crumbled
sea salt and freshly ground black pepper

Heat a pan over a medium heat and add the oil and butter. Once the butter is melted and foaming, add the celery and onion. Cook for 2–3 minutes, until the onion has softened and the celery is tender, tossing the pan occasionally. Pour in the port and wine, then flambé it off a little by tipping the edge of the pan over the flames very carefully. When the alcohol burns off, stir in the stock and slowly add the cream, then tip in the cheese. Simmer for about 20 minutes, until reduced, thickened and darkened in colour. Season to taste and use as required. This will keep covered in the fridge for 3–4 days.

Wild Mushroom Butter

1 tbsp olive oil
1 shallot, finely diced
1 garlic clove, crushed
50g (2oz) mixed wild mushrooms, roughly chopped (such as cep, chanterelle, shiitake and oyster)
1 tbsp Madeira
1 tbsp cream
1 tsp chopped fresh flat-leaf parsley
½ tsp chopped fresh thyme
100g (4oz) butter, diced (at room temperature)
sea salt and freshly ground black pepper

Heat the olive oil in a pan over a medium heat and add the shallot, garlic and mushrooms. Cook gently for 5 minutes, until cooked through and tender but not coloured. Stir in the Madeira, cream and herbs and cook for a further 3 minutes, until the liquid has completely reduced and evaporated. Season to taste and leave to cool, then place in a food processor with the butter and purée until smooth. Using a spatula, scrape out onto a square of parchment paper and roll into a cylinder about 2.5cm (1in) thick, twisting the ends to secure. Chill for at least 2 hours to harden. Use as required. This will keep for up to 2 weeks in the fridge or it can be frozen.

Whiskey Sauce
Makes 325ml (11fl oz)

25g (1oz) butter
1 tbsp olive oil
150g (5oz) button mushrooms, sliced
1 shallot, finely chopped
120ml (4fl oz) Irish whiskey
150ml (¼ pint) white wine
150ml (¼ pint) beef stock (page 227)
150ml (¼ pint) cream
1 tbsp Worcestershire sauce
good pinch of sugar
1 tbsp chopped fresh flat-leaf parsley
squeeze of lemon juice
sea salt and freshly ground black pepper

Heat a pan over a medium heat and add the butter and oil, then swirl until the butter has melted and is foaming. Tip in the mushrooms and shallot and sauté for 2–3 minutes, until tender. Pour over the whiskey, then use a match or tilt up the pan to catch the flame. It will flare up for 5–10 seconds and then subside when the alcohol burns off. Add the white wine, stirring to combine, then simmer for 6–8 minutes, until reduced by half. Stir in the stock, cream, Worcestershire sauce and sugar. Bring to the boil, then reduce the heat and simmer for 20–25 minutes, stirring occasionally, until thickened and reduced to a sauce consistency that will coat the back of a wooden spoon. Stir in the parsley and lemon juice and season to taste. Use as required. This will keep covered in the fridge for 3–4 days.

Peppered Shallot Butter

1 tsp sunflower oil
3 shallots, very finely chopped
100g (4oz) butter, softened
1 tbsp black peppercorns, coarsely
  crushed
1 tsp Dijon mustard
¼ tsp sea salt flakes

Heat the oil in a small pan over a medium heat, then add the shallots and gently fry for 6–8 minutes, until golden brown. Leave to cool, then beat into the butter with the pepper-corns, mustard and salt. Scrape out onto a square of parchment paper and roll into a cylinder 2.5cm (1in) thick, twisting the ends to secure. Chill for at least 2 hours to harden. Use as required.

Beef Wellington

This is a wonderful, classic dish that no one ever seems to tire of and keeps the cost of fillet steak to a minimum. It can be made up to 12 hours in advance and kept covered in the fridge until needed. Just remember to give it a little longer in the oven if you are using it straight from the fridge. Serves 6

olive oil
75g (3oz) unsalted butter
800g (1 ¾lb) piece of centre-cut beef fillet, at room temperature
75g (3oz) shallots, finely diced
150g (5oz) flat mushrooms, finely chopped
2 tbsp cream
1 tbsp chopped fresh flat-leaf parsley
1 egg yolk
1 tbsp milk

2 x 375g (13oz) packets ready-rolled puff pastry, thawed
4 ready-made pancakes (crêpes)
175g (6oz) chicken liver pâté (home-made, pages 22–3, or shop-bought)
sea salt and freshly ground black pepper
Madeira sauce (page 230), to serve
steamed baby carrots, to serve
steamed baby new potatoes, to serve

Heat the oil and 15g (½oz) of the butter in a frying pan over a medium heat and season the beef. Add the beef and quickly seal all over. Remove from the pan, place on a plate and allow to cool completely.

To make the stuffing, heat the rest of the butter in the frying pan until foaming. Add the shallots and cook for 5 minutes, until lightly golden, then add the mushrooms and cook for another 3–4 minutes, stirring until all the liquid evaporates. Stir in the cream and season, then cook for a few minutes more, until reduced to a thick paste. Stir in the parsley and cool.

Mix the egg yolk with the milk in a bowl and set aside. Unroll one of the packets of pastry onto a large baking sheet lined with parchment paper and lay 2 pancakes on top, slightly overlapping. Spread the pâté in a strip across the centre of the pancakes, to the same width as the beef.

Make a lengthways cut into the centre of the beef about three-quarters of the way through and fill with the mushroom stuffing. Place the beef on the pancakes and cover with the 2 remaining pancakes, slightly overlapping. Tuck the bottom pancakes up the sides of the beef and under the top pancakes. Brush the egg wash around the pastry edges and lay the second sheet of puff pastry on top, trimming down as necessary, then press down the edges to seal with the tip of a teaspoon. Decorate with the pastry trimmings and brush with the egg wash. Place in the fridge for 20 minutes. Preheat the oven to 230°C (450°F/gas mark 8).

Place in the oven for 10 minutes, then reduce the heat to 190°C (375°F/gas mark 5) for another 20 minutes, until the pastry is puffed up and golden. Leave to rest on a carving board for 15 minutes.

To serve, carve the beef Wellington into thick slices and arrange on warmed serving plates with Madeira sauce, baby carrots and baby new potatoes.

CHICKEN

When you're in the mood for a real winter warmer that has tons of flavour, appeals to all the family and takes very little time to get in the oven compared to traditional casseroles, you can't go far wrong with this recipe. Serves 6–8

12 rindless streaky bacon rashers
12 skinless, boneless chicken thighs
3 tbsp rapeseed oil
2 onions, cut into wedges
2 sweet potatoes, peeled and cut into cubes
2 garlic cloves, crushed
275g (10oz) flat mushrooms, sliced
2 tbsp redcurrant jelly
finely grated rind of 1 orange
1 bay leaf
450ml (¾ pint) chicken stock (page 226)
120ml (4fl oz) dry cider
2 tsp fresh thyme leaves
1 tbsp chopped fresh flat-leaf parsley
1 tbsp toasted flaked almonds
sea salt and freshly ground black pepper
creamy mashed potatoes, to serve (page 151)

Preheat the oven to 200°C (400°F/gas mark 6).

Stretch each rasher with the back of a table knife and then wrap it around a chicken thigh. Heat the oil in a large casserole with a lid and cook the wrapped chicken thighs in batches until lightly browned all over. Arrange on a plate and set aside.

Reduce the heat, then add the onions and sweet potatoes. Sauté for 5 minutes, until golden. Add the garlic and cook for 1 minute, stirring to prevent it from sticking.

Add the mushrooms, redcurrant jelly, orange rind and bay leaf then pour in the stock and cider. Bring to the boil, then reduce the heat, return the chicken to the casserole and stir in the thyme. Cover and cook for 1 hour, or until the chicken is completely tender and the sauce has thickened slightly. Season to taste and stir in the parsley.

To serve, sprinkle the casserole with the flaked almonds, then place directly on the table with a large bowl of creamy mashed potatoes to mop up all those delicious juices.

Pesto-stuffed Chicken Breasts with Rustic Mixed Potatoes

I always make my own pesto, which literally takes minutes, with basil, toasted pine nuts, garlic, Parmesan and olive oil (see the recipe on page 228), or buy a good-quality one. These ultra trendy potato slices not only go well with these pesto-stuffed chicken breasts, but are great as a side dish for a barbecue. They can be made in large quantities in trays and simply reheated as necessary. Serves 4

125g (4 ½oz) ball of mozzarella, torn into small pieces
4 tbsp basil pesto (page 228 or shop bought)
4 skinless, boneless chicken breast fillets
8 cherry tomatoes, halved
8 smoked streaky bacon rashers, rinds removed
sea salt and freshly ground black pepper
steamed French green beans, to serve

Rustic mixed potatoes:
450g (1lb) Rooster potatoes, scrubbed
225g (8oz) sweet potatoes, scrubbed
3 garlic cloves, lightly crushed (skin still on)
1 fresh rosemary sprig, broken into tiny sprigs
sea salt flakes
2 tbsp olive oil

Preheat the oven to 200°C (400°F/gas mark 6).

Mix together the mozzarella and pesto. Cut a slit into the side of each chicken breast and then stuff with the pesto-covered cheese. Place 2 halved cherry tomatoes in each breast. Wrap each stuffed chicken breast with 2 bacon rashers – not too tightly, but enough to hold the chicken together. Season with salt and pepper.

To make the rustic mixed potatoes, cut the potatoes and sweet potatoes into 5mm (¼in) slices – a Japanese mandolin is perfect for doing this – and arrange in a single layer on a large roasting tray lined with parchment paper. Add the garlic and rosemary and season with salt. Drizzle over the oil and toss until evenly coated.

Nestle the pesto-stuffed chicken breasts in the potatoes and roast for 20–25 minutes, until the chicken is cooked through and the bacon is crispy. Remove the chicken from the oven and rest in a warm place for 5 minutes. Return the potatoes to the oven in that time for a final crisp-up.

To serve, arrange the pesto-stuffed chicken breasts on warmed serving plates with steamed French green beans and the rustic mixed potatoes.

Spicy Chicken Salad with Mango Salsa

This is a great rustic salad that everyone seems to enjoy. The chicken can be prepared well in advance, ready to deep-fry at the last minute. If you don't fancy the mango salsa, try serving it with an avocado and tomato salsa. Serves 4

4 slices of day-old white bread, crusts
  removed
2 tsp medium curry powder
2 tsp mild chilli powder
2 tsp sesame seeds
1 tbsp chopped fresh flat-leaf parsley
50g (2oz) plain flour
2 eggs
2 tbsp milk
4 skinless chicken breast fillets, cut into
  strips lengthways
vegetable oil, for deep-frying
100g (4oz) mixed baby salad leaves
1–2 tbsp rapeseed oil

1 tsp balsamic vinegar
sea salt and freshly ground black pepper
balsamic cream, to serve (page 230)

Mango salsa:
1 ripe mango, peeled and finely diced
  (stone removed)
1 small roasted red pepper, peeled,
  seeded and diced
finely grated rind and juice of 1 lime
2 tbsp sweet chilli sauce
1 tbsp rapeseed oil
1 tbsp chopped fresh coriander
1 tbsp chopped fresh basil

To make the mango salsa, place the mango in a bowl and stir in the roasted red pepper, lime rind and juice, sweet chilli sauce, oil, coriander and basil. Season to taste. Cover with clingfilm and set aside at room temperature until needed.

Place the bread in a food processor or liquidiser and whizz to fine crumbs. With the motor still running, add the curry powder, chilli powder, sesame seeds and parsley and blend until just combined. Tip into a shallow dish and season well.

Place the flour on a plate. Beat the eggs and milk together in another shallow dish. Toss the chicken strips in the flour until well coated, shaking off any excess, then dip into the egg mixture and coat in the flavoured breadcrumbs.

Heat a deep-fat fryer to 160°C (325°F) or half-fill a deep-sided pan with vegetable oil. Cook the breaded chicken strips in batches for 6–8 minutes, or until cooked through and golden brown. Drain on kitchen paper and keep warm in a low oven while you cook the rest.

Meanwhile, dress the salad leaves with the rapeseed oil and balsamic vinegar and season to taste.

To serve, spoon a little balsamic cream into the middle of each warmed serving plate and add a mound of the spicy chicken. Spoon the mango salsa around the outside and put the dressed salad leaves on top.

Sticky Chicken Wings with Asian Slaw

This dish can be cooked in the oven at any time, but there's no doubt that the chicken wings taste fantastic when they've been cooked outdoors on a barbecue, so get some in next time the temperatures are set to rise. **Serves 4**

50g (2oz) light muscovado sugar
3 tbsp hot chilli sauce
2 tbsp balsamic vinegar
2 tbsp dark soy sauce
1 tsp wholegrain mustard
32 chicken wings, well trimmed
fresh coriander sprigs, to garnish
  (optional)

Asian slaw:
juice of 1 lime
4 tbsp rapeseed oil

2 tbsp sesame oil
2 tbsp chopped fresh coriander
1 tbsp toasted sesame seeds
1 tbsp light soy sauce
1 heaped tsp freshly grated root ginger
1 carrot, cut into thin strips
1 small red onion, thinly sliced
175g (6oz) white cabbage, core removed
  and finely shredded
50g (2oz) watercress, well picked over
sea salt and freshly ground black pepper

Place the sugar, hot chilli sauce, balsamic vinegar, soy sauce and mustard in a shallow, non-metallic dish with the chicken wings and mix well to combine. Cover with clingfilm and chill for at least 3 hours, or better still, overnight.

Preheat the oven to 190°C (375°F/gas mark 5).

Give the chicken wings a good mix to ensure that the marinade is evenly distributed and then tip them into a large roasting tin. Bake for 25–30 minutes, or until cooked through and slightly charred and sticky on the outside.

To make the dressing, place the lime juice in a bowl with the rapeseed oil, sesame oil, coriander, sesame seeds, soy sauce and ginger and then whisk to combine. Season to taste.

Place the carrot, red onion and cabbage in a large bowl and toss gently to combine. Drizzle over enough of the dressing to coat.

To serve, fold the watercress into the slaw and pile into a serving bowl. Arrange the sticky chicken wings in a separate warmed serving bowl and drizzle over any sauce left from the tin. Serve straight to the table and have plenty of napkins to hand for all those sticky

Fragrant Roast Chicken with Sausage Stuffing

There is something very comforting about a whole roast chicken brought to the table – it reminds me of family Sunday lunches from childhood. The flavours here are fantastic and really penetrate the flesh of the chicken. Try to buy a free-range or organic chicken, as the flavour is always so much better. Serves 4–6

1.5kg (3lb) whole chicken
1 lemon
1 fresh thyme sprig
75g (3oz) butter, softened
2 garlic cloves, crushed
4 small carrots, peeled
2 red onions, peeled and halved
2 celery sticks, chopped in half
1 leek, chopped in half
1 garlic bulb, broken into cloves (but not peeled)
3 tbsp olive oil
1 tbsp plain flour
120ml (4fl oz) white wine
300ml (½ pint) chicken stock (page 226)
sea salt and freshly ground black pepper
crispy roast potatoes, to serve (page 152)
buttered peas, to serve

Sausage stuffing roll:
25g (1oz) butter, extra for greasing
1 onion, finely chopped
100g (4oz) sausage meat
100g (4oz) fresh white breadcrumbs
2 tbsp chopped fresh herbs, such as flat-leaf parsley, sage, rosemary and thyme

Take the chicken out of the fridge 30 minutes before it goes into the oven. Preheat the oven to 230°C (450°F/gas mark 8).

Finely grate the rind from the lemon and place the rind in a bowl, reserving the lemon. Strip the thyme leaves from the stalks (reserve the stalks) and add to the lemon rind. Mix in the butter and the garlic and then season to taste.

Loosen the skin from the chicken breasts, starting at the cavity end and working your hand underneath to release it. Spread the butter evenly under the skin and lay the skin back down on top. Slash the chicken legs several times with a sharp knife (this is to help ensure crispy skin).

Place the carrots in a roasting tin with the red onions, celery, leek and garlic, tossing to coat in 1 tablespoon of olive oil. Sit the chicken on top of the pile of vegetables and drizzle all over with the remaining 2 tablespoons olive oil, then season well, rubbing it all over and right into the slashes.

Cut the reserved lemon in half and put it inside the chicken's cavity with the reserved thyme stalks. Place the chicken in the oven and immediately reduce the heat to 200°C (400°F/gas mark 6). Roast the chicken for 1 hour 20 minutes, basting the chicken halfway through cooking.

Meanwhile, to make the sausage stuffing roll, melt the butter in a frying pan and sauté the onion until softened. Leave to cool, then mix with the sausage meat, breadcrumbs and herbs and season with salt and pepper. Place on a heavily buttered double sheet of tin foil and roll up into a thick sausage shape about 2.5cm (1in) thick and 20cm (8in) long, twisting the ends to secure. Place in a roasting tin and cook above the chicken for 25–30 minutes, until the sausage meat is cooked through, turning it a couple of times to ensure it cooks evenly.

When the chicken is cooked, transfer the chicken to a board and put the carrots and red onions on a warmed plate. Cover each with tin foil and rest for 15 minutes while you make the gravy.

Using a large spoon, carefully remove most of the fat from the tin and then place the tin directly on the heat. Stir in the flour and then holding the tin steady, mash up the remaining vegetables as much as possible with a potato masher. Pour in the wine and allow it to bubble down, stirring continuously to blend the flour in. Pour in the stock and bring to the boil, then reduce the heat and simmer for about 10 minutes, until slightly reduced and thickened, stirring occasionally. Take a large jug and set a sieve into it, then pour in the gravy mixture, using a ladle to push all of the liquid and some of the vegetables through with the back of the spoon. Stir in the juices from the resting chicken and season to taste. Transfer to a warmed gravy boat.

To serve, carve the chicken into slices and arrange on warmed serving plates with the reserved carrots and red onion halves. Unwrap the sausage stuffing roll and cut into slices, then add to the plates with the roast potatoes and buttered peas. Hand around the gravy boat separately.

LAMB

Braised Lamb Shanks with Carrots

Ask your butcher to trim off any excess fat from the lamb shanks and remove the knuckles, as that can be a difficult job. Although now popular restaurant fare, lamb shanks are still good value for money so it's well worth seeking them out. **Serves 6**

1 tbsp rapeseed oil
6 lamb shanks, well trimmed and knuckles removed
4 celery sticks, sliced
4 garlic cloves, peeled
1 onion, roughly chopped
75g (3oz) plain flour
1 fresh thyme sprig
1 fresh rosemary sprig
2 litres (3 ½ pints) beef stock (page 227)
600ml (1 pint) red wine
1 tbsp tomato purée
200g (7oz) carrots, cut into wedges
sea salt and freshly ground black pepper
champ, to serve (page 151)
chopped fresh flat-leaf parsley, to garnish

Preheat the oven to 160°C (325°F/gas mark 3).

Heat the oil in a large casserole (that has a lid) over a high heat. Add the lamb shanks and fry until lightly browned on all sides, turning regularly. Transfer to a plate. Add the celery, garlic and onion to the pan and sauté for 5 minutes, until lightly golden. Stir in the flour to coat.

Return the lamb shanks to the casserole with the thyme and rosemary sprigs. Pour over the stock and wine to cover, then stir in the tomato purée. Season and cover tightly with foil and then the lid. Cook in the oven for 1 ½ hours. Remove the casserole from the oven, add the carrots and cook for 1 hour more, until the lamb is very tender and almost falling off the bone.

Strain the cooking liquid into a separate pan and then put the lid back on the casserole to keep the lamb shanks warm. Bring the cooking liquid to a simmer, then cook until reduced to a sauce consistency. Season to taste.

To serve, spoon the champ onto warmed serving plates and arrange a lamb shank on top of each one. Spoon the vegetables to the side and drizzle around the reduced sauce. Garnish with the flat-leaf parsley.

Lamb Cutlets with Garlic, Lemon and Paprika

This marinade is wonderful with lamb and would also work well with any type of lamb leg steaks or sideloin chops, depending on what is available. Lamb cutlets are that bit more expensive, but they take no time to cook. The longer you can marinade this, the better the flavour, so it's well worth preparing in advance. Serves 4

2 garlic cloves, crushed
finely grated rind and juice of 1 lemon
2 tbsp rapeseed oil
2 tsp smoked paprika
2 tsp chopped fresh oregano or thyme
1 tsp clear honey
12 lamb cutlets, well trimmed
sea salt and freshly ground black pepper
peach, feta cheese and rocket salad, to serve
steamed baby new potatoes, to serve

Place the garlic, lemon rind and juice, oil, paprika, herbs, honey and some salt and pepper in a shallow non-metallic dish. Stir until well combined. Add the lamb, turning to coat, then set aside for at least 10 minutes, or up to 24 hours, covered with clingfilm in the fridge if time allows.

When you're ready to cook, light the barbecue, preheat a grill to medium or heat a griddle pan. Shake the excess marinade from the lamb. Put the lamb on the barbecue on medium-hot coals or arrange on a grill rack or a griddle pan. Cook for 6–8 minutes, until cooked through, turning once. Remove from the heat and leave the lamb cutlets to rest for a couple of minutes.

To serve, arrange the lamb cutlets on warmed serving plates with the peach, feta and rocket salad and some steamed baby new potatoes.

Irish Stew

I never tire of a bowl of steaming hot Irish stew, but it's the attention to detail that makes this dish one of the world's great classics. This is my version, which I have developed over the years. Some people say you shouldn't use carrots, but this began as one of my mother's recipes and I'm still putting carrots in! Ask your local craft butcher for some neck or shoulder cuts. If you make it the day before and warm it up, your meal will be more tender. We serve a small portion of this stew in the restaurant in a dish featuring 4 versions of cooked lamb. Serves 6

900g (2lb) boneless lamb neck, trimmed and cut into cubes
1 litre (1 ¾ pints) chicken stock (page 226)
50g (2oz) pearl barley, washed
225g (8oz) potatoes, cut into chunks
225g (8oz) carrots, thickly sliced
225g (8oz) leeks, well trimmed and thickly sliced
225g (8oz) baby pearl onions or small shallots, peeled
2 fresh thyme sprigs
sea salt and freshly ground black pepper
chopped fresh parsley, to garnish
colcannon, to serve (page 151)

Place the lamb in a large, heavy-based pan and pour over the stock. Bring to the boil, then skim off any scum from the surface and stir in the barley. Reduce the heat and simmer for 50 minutes, until slightly reduced and the lamb is almost tender.

Add the potatoes to the lamb with the carrots, leeks, baby pearl onions and thyme and simmer for 30 minutes, or until the lamb and vegetables are completely tender but still holding their shape. Season to taste.

To serve, transfer the stew into a warmed casserole dish and scatter over the parsley. Have a dish of colcannon alongside and allow everyone to help themselves.

Roast Leg of Spring Lamb with Boulangère Potatoes

This dish is hassle free – perfect for a dinner party or Sunday lunch. **Serves 6**

1 tbsp rapeseed oil
knob of butter
3 onions, thinly sliced
1.5kg (3lb) potatoes, peeled and thinly sliced
4 fresh thyme sprigs, leaves stripped
400ml (14fl oz) chicken stock (page 226)
1.75kg (4lb) leg of lamb
3 garlic cloves, sliced
2 fresh rosemary sprigs
sea salt and freshly ground black pepper
wilted spinach (page 225), to serve

Preheat the oven to 200°C (400°F/gas mark 6).

To make the boulangère potatoes, heat the oil in a frying pan with the butter and sauté the onions for 3–4 minutes over a medium heat, until softened but not coloured. Season to taste. Layer the potatoes, onions and thyme leaves in a large roasting tin large enough to fit the leg of lamb. Season each layer as you go and finish with an attractive overlapping layer of the potatoes. Pour over the stock and set to one side.

Using a sharp knife, make small incisions all over the lamb and press a garlic slice and a tiny sprig of the rosemary into each one. Weigh the joint and allow 20 minutes per 450g (1lb) plus 20 minutes (add a further 20 minutes for well done), then place the lamb carefully on top of the potatoes in the roasting tin. Roast for 20 minutes, then reduce the oven temperature to 180°C (350°F/gas mark 4) and roast for 1 hour 20 minutes for a leg of lamb this size (1.75kg (4lb)).

Transfer the leg of lamb to a carving platter and cover loosely with foil, then leave to rest for 15 minutes, keeping the boulangère potatoes warm.

To serve, carve the lamb into slices and arrange on warmed serving plates with the boulangère potatoes and wilted spinach.

Shepherd's Pie

This recipe can be prepared a day in advance or made up and frozen until needed. It also works very well with minced beef, although my personal favourite is with lamb. Serves 4

1 tbsp rapeseed oil
450g (1lb) lean minced lamb
2 smoked bacon rashers, rind removed
  and diced
4 carrots, diced
1 onion, chopped
1 garlic clove, crushed
2 tbsp Worcestershire sauce
300ml (½ pint) chicken stock (page 226)
  or beef stock (page 227)
1 tbsp tomato purée

1 tsp chopped fresh thyme
100g (4oz) frozen garden peas, thawed
1 tbsp chopped fresh flat-leaf parsley
sea salt and freshly ground black pepper
buttered peas, to serve

Cheesy mash:
900g (2lb) floury potatoes, cut into cubes
50g (2oz) mature Cheddar cheese, grated
25g (1oz) butter
100ml (3 ½fl oz) warm milk

Heat a large saucepan and add the oil. Tip in the mince and smoked bacon and sauté for about 5 minutes, until browned all over, breaking up any lumps with a wooden spoon. Remove from the pan with a slotted spoon and set aside. Add in the carrots, onion and garlic and cook for 4–5 minutes, until just starting to change colour.

Stir the Worcestershire sauce into the vegetables, then add the stock, tomato purée and thyme along with the sautéed minced lamb. Mix well to combine, then cover and simmer for 20 minutes, until the mince is completely tender and cooked through. Finally, stir in the peas and parsley and season to taste. Place the cooked mince into an ovenproof dish and leave to cool slightly for about 20 minutes.

Preheat the oven to 180°C (350°F/gas mark 4).

To make the cheesy mash, gently steam the potatoes until tender. Mash well, making sure there are no lumps. Beat in the cheese, butter and milk and season to taste. Gently spoon the cheesy mash on top of the mince, spreading it with a fork in an even manner. Cook in the oven for 30–40 minutes, until the cheesy mash is golden brown.

To serve, place the shepherd's pie straight on the table with a separate bowl of buttered peas and allow everyone to help themselves.

PORK

Caramelised Pork Belly with Honey and Ginger Sauce

Ask your butcher for pieces of pork belly that are between 5–7.5cm (2–3in) thick. The best ones come from the front belly for a good balance of meat and fat. The way to tell is to look at how much lean meat is layered with the fat and choose a slab that's about 50/50 lean to fat and ensure that it is well trimmed down. This dish works best if you start it 24 hours in advance. **Serves 6**

2 tbsp rapeseed oil
1.5kg (3lb) pork belly, boned and rolled
2 carrots, diced
1 onion, diced
1.2 litres (2 pints) beef stock (page 227)
600ml (1 pint) red wine
600ml (1 pint) freshly pressed apple juice
2 garlic cloves, crushed
2 fresh thyme sprigs
2 fresh rosemary sprigs

1 tsp softened butter
4 tbsp clear honey
4 tbsp dark soy sauce
2 star anise
wilted spinach (page 225), to serve
honey and ginger sauce (page 229), to serve
creamy mashed potatoes (page 151), to serve

Preheat the oven to 160°C (325°F/gas mark 3). Heat 1 tablespoon of oil in a heavy-based pan over a medium heat. Add the pork belly and brown all over, turning regularly with tongs. Transfer to a casserole dish. Add the carrots and onion to the pan and cook for a further 5 minutes, until golden brown, stirring regularly to ensure they cook evenly.

Tip the vegetables over the seared pork belly and stir in the beef stock, red wine, apple juice, garlic and herbs. Cover tightly with a lid or foil and bake for 3 hours, until the pork belly is meltingly tender. Remove from the oven and leave to sit for 1 hour in the braising juices, then remove, cut the string and wrap twice in tin foil. Reserve the braising juices to use in the sauce. This is all best done 24 hours in advance.

To reheat the pork belly, put a large frying pan on a medium heat with the remaining tablespoon of oil and the butter. Cut the pork into 12 even-sized slices and arrange in a single layer in the heated frying pan – you may have to do this in batches. Cook for 2–3 minutes on each side, until just golden. Transfer to a plate and keep warm. Add the honey, soy sauce and star anise to the pan and allow to bubble down for 1–2 minutes, until syrupy. Return the pieces of pork belly to the pan and cook for another 3–4 minutes, basting regularly, until sticky and caramelised.

To serve, place 2 slices of the caramelised pork belly on each warmed serving plate and add some wilted spinach. Spoon the honey and ginger sauce alongside the pork belly and serve the mashed potatoes in a separate warmed dish.

Bacon and Cabbage with Parsley Sauce

If your bacon is very salty, there will be a white froth on top of the water, in which case it's better to discard the water and start again. It can be necessary to change the water several times, depending on how salty the bacon is. Choose a joint with a nice covering of fat for the best flavour. Any leftovers are delicious reheated – simply arrange in a roasting tin with a splash of water and cover with foil, then pop into a preheated oven at 180°C (350°F/gas mark 4) for 10–15 minutes, until warmed through. **Serves 8–10**

2.25kg (5lb) pork loin, collar or streaky bacon with rind on (smoked or unsmoked)
1 Savoy cabbage or 2 spring cabbages
50g (2oz) butter
sea salt and freshly ground black pepper
steamed turnip with a knob of butter, to serve (optional)

Parsley sauce:
600ml (1 pint) milk
1 fresh thyme sprig
½ onion, sliced
handful of fresh flat-leaf parsley, leaves finely chopped and stalks reserved
25g (1oz) butter
25g (1oz) plain flour

Place the bacon in a large pan and cover with cold water. Bring slowly to the boil and change the water as necessary (see the introduction). Cover with a lid and simmer until almost cooked, allowing 20 minutes per 450g (1lb).

Meanwhile, trim away the outer leaves of the cabbage. Cut it into quarters and remove the core. Slice the cabbage across the grain into thick shreds. About 3–4 minutes before the end of the bacon's cooking time, add the shredded cabbage. Stir, then cover and continue to simmer gently until both the cabbage and bacon are cooked (about 1 ¾ hours in total).

To make the parsley sauce, put the milk in a pan with the thyme, onion and parsley stalks. Bring to a simmer, season to taste and simmer for 4–5 minutes. Remove from the heat and leave to infuse for 30 minutes if time allows, then strain through a sieve.

Melt the butter in a clean pan and stir in the flour. Cook for 1 minute, stirring, and then gradually add the infused milk, whisking to combine. Continue to simmer until the sauce has slightly thickened, then season to taste and stir in the chopped parsley leaves. If not using immediately, remove from the heat and set aside until needed.

Remove the bacon from the pan and cut off the rind, if liked. Strain the cabbage and discard the water (or if it's not too salty, keep it for soup). Add the butter to the cabbage and season with pepper.

To serve, carve the bacon into slices and arrange on warmed serving plates with the buttered cabbage and drizzle over a little of the parsley sauce. Put the rest of the parsley sauce into a warmed gravy boat and serve at the table so everyone can help themselves. Have a separate warmed serving dish of steamed turnip with a knob of butter melting in it, if liked.

Bacon and Cabbage with Parsley Sauce

Marinated Pork Fillet with Sausage Stuffing

Marinated Pork Fillet with Sausage Stuffing

This recipe is based on a dish that I was taught to cook in college. It's always been a favourite in our house and when I made it again recently, I was surprised at how good it was – I had forgotten. The meat really does need to be marinated overnight to achieve the best flavour. Serves 4

1 pork tenderloin (fillet), about 675g (1 ½lb) in total
freshly ground black pepper
2 garlic cloves, crushed
2 tbsp light soy sauce
2 tbsp rapeseed oil
1 tbsp light muscovado sugar
2 tsp freshly grated root ginger
1 tsp mild curry powder
good pinch of ground cinnamon
sea salt and freshly ground black pepper
buttered noodles with roasted peppers and coriander, to serve
red wine sauce (page 230), to serve

Sausage stuffing:
200g (7oz) good-quality sausage meat
1 egg
2 tbsp Ballymaloe jalapeño relish
1 tbsp chopped fresh basil, plus sprigs to garnish
2 tsp snipped fresh chives
100ml (3 ½fl oz) cream
2 tbsp toasted pine nuts

Trim away any fat and membrane from the pork tenderloin and split it lengthways, without cutting right through. Open it out flat and season generously with pepper. Cover with clingfilm and flatten out the sides using a mallet, rolling pin or the base of a pan, being careful not to put any holes in the meat. Try to keep the shape as rectangular as possible with a thickness of no more than 1cm (½in).

To prepare the marinade, place the garlic, soy sauce, oil, sugar, ginger, curry powder and cinnamon in a shallow non-metallic dish that's large enough to fit the pork tenderloin comfortably. Stir until well combined and then add the pork fillet, turning to coat. Cover with clingfilm and chill for at least 4 hours, or up to 24 hours is great, to allow the flavours to penetrate the meat.

To make the stuffing, place the sausage meat in a food processor with the egg, relish, basil and chives. Blend until smooth and then slowly add the cream through the feeder tube. Season generously and then blend again for 2 minutes. Transfer to a bowl and mix in the toasted pine nuts, then cover with clingfilm and chill for at least 1 hour to firm up (or up to the same amount of time as the pork).

When ready to cook, preheat the oven to 200°C (400°F/gas mark 6).

Remove the marinated pork tenderloin from the fridge and place on a large sheet of tin foil. Spoon the sausage meat down the centre of the pork, then using the tin foil, carefully roll the pork tenderloin over the sausage stuffing to enclose. Twist the ends of the foil tightly and place the pork on a large baking sheet lined with parchment paper. Roast for 50 minutes, turning occasionally, until cooked through and firm to the touch.

Remove the pork tenderloin parcel from the oven and leave to rest for 5 minutes, then carefully remove the tin foil. Slice the pork on a chopping board and carve into slices 1cm (½in) thick and arrange on plates on beds of the buttered noodles with roasted peppers and coriander. Drizzle around the red wine sauce and garnish with basil to serve.

Fragrant Pork and Pumpkin Curry

I first tasted curried pork in coconut milk in Thailand, which is one of my favourite places. This is not an overly spicy dish, so it's good for introducing children to Asian foods and widening their palate. Look out for kaffir lime leaves, which come fresh, frozen or dried. Fresh are best, and any that you don't use can be kept in the freezer for another day.
Serves 4–6

50g (2oz) Thai red curry paste (from a jar)
1kg (2 ¼lb) pork shoulder, trimmed and cut into cubes
8 kaffir lime leaves, lightly crushed (optional)
500ml (18fl oz) chicken stock (page 226)
2 x 250ml (9fl oz) cartons coconut cream
1 tbsp freshly grated root ginger
675g (1 ½lb) pumpkin, peeled, seeded and cut into cubes
2 tbsp fresh lime juice
1 tbsp Thai fish sauce (nam pla)
1 tbsp light muscovado sugar
steamed Thai fragrant rice or basmati rice, to serve
25g (1oz) fresh coriander leaves, to garnish
25g (1oz) fresh mint leaves, to garnish
2 spring onions, trimmed and shredded, to garnish
2 limes, cut into wedges, to garnish

Heat a wok or a large, deep, non-stick frying pan over a medium to high heat. Add the curry paste and cook for 1 minute, until fragrant. Add the pork and cook, stirring, for 4 minutes, or until the pork is well coated. Add the lime leaves (if using), stock, coconut cream and ginger and simmer, covered, for 25 minutes. Add the pumpkin and cover and simmer for another 15 minutes, or until the pork and pumpkin are tender. Stir through the lime juice, fish sauce and sugar.

To serve, divide the pork and pumpkin curry among serving bowls with the rice in a separate warmed serving bowl. Serve to the table with separate dishes of the coriander, mint, shredded spring onions and lime wedges so that guests can garnish the curry themselves.

Pork Cutlets with Roasted Apple

These pork chops are roasted until they're beautifully golden but still tender and moist. They would also be delicious done on the barbecue or under the grill. Serves 4

1 small orange
1 tbsp rapeseed oil
1 tsp prepared English mustard
1 tsp chopped fresh rosemary
4 loin pork chops (on the bone)
1 eating apple
1 tsp fresh oregano leaves
50g (2oz) butter, melted
sea salt and freshly ground black pepper
jacket potatoes, to serve
steamed greens, to serve

Finely grate the rind from the orange into a bowl and then squeeze in the juice. Whisk in the oil, mustard and rosemary. Season to taste and pour into a shallow non-metallic dish. Using a small, sharp knife, score the fat and rind of the pork chops, then add to the marinade, turning to coat. Cover with clingfilm and set aside for at least 10 minutes, or up to 24 hours in the fridge is great, to allow the flavours to penetrate the meat.

When you are ready to cook, preheat the oven to 220°C (425°F/gas mark 7). Line a baking sheet with parchment paper.

Shake off the excess marinade from the pork and place the chops on the lined baking sheet. Cut the apple into slices and arrange 3 slices on each cutlet. Scatter over the oregano and then brush with melted butter. Roast for 20 minutes, until the pork is cooked through and tender and the apple is golden. Remove from the heat and leave to rest for a couple of minutes.

To serve, arrange the pork cutlets with roasted apple on warmed serving plates with the jacket potatoes. Have a bowl of steamed greens to hand around separately.

FISH

Pan-fried Fish with Lemon and Herb Butter Sauce

Buy fish that has been prepared as much as possible: whole fish should be gutted and, if necessary, scaled, then filleted and all the bones removed. This leaves you with no work to do at home. It is essential not to overcook fish – pan-frying is probably the easiest way to get successful results every time. I just love the simplicity of this recipe or any of the variations on page 80. **Serves 4**

4 x 175g (6oz) firm white fish fillets (such as hake, haddock,
    whiting, cod, pollock or coley), skin on and boned
1 tbsp olive oil
50g (2oz) butter
1 tbsp chopped fresh mixed herbs (flat-leaf parsley, chives and tarragon)
squeeze of fresh lemon juice
sea salt and freshly ground black pepper
steamed mangetout, to serve
sautéed new potatoes, to serve

Season the fish fillets with salt and pepper. Heat the olive oil in a large frying pan over a medium heat and add the fish, skin side down. Cook for 1–2 minutes, until the skin is just beginning to crisp, then add a little knob of the butter to the pan around each fillet and cook for another couple of minutes, until the skin is crisp.

Turn the fish fillets over and cook for another 3–4 minutes, until cooked through. This will depend on the thickness of the fillets. Transfer to warmed serving plates while you make the sauce.

Add the rest of the butter to the frying pan that you have cooked the fish in and allow it to melt over a moderate heat. Quickly add the herbs and a squeeze of lemon juice, swirling to combine. Season to taste.

To serve, spoon the lemon and herb butter sauce over the fish fillets and add the mangetout. Serve a separate warmed dish of the sautéed new potatoes to each plate.

Variations

Bacon and Lemon

The combination of fish and bacon may not be an obvious one, but it really is a winner. Use dry-cured streaky bacon if possible. Remove the rind, then cut into cubes and fry until sizzling before making the butter sauce. Season to taste and use as required.

Mustard

Add 100ml (3 ½fl oz) of cream to the frying pan that you have cooked the fish in and allow to reduce down to a sauce consistency, then stir in 1 teaspoon of your favourite mustard and a sprinkling of chopped fresh chives. Season to taste and use as required.

White Wine and Crème Fraîche

Add a glass of white wine to the frying pan that you have cooked the fish in and allow to reduce down to a sticky glaze, scraping the bottom of the pan to remove any sediment. Stir in 4 tablespoons of crème fraîche and allow to reduce down a little, then add the herbs and lemon as above. Season to taste and use as required.

Seafood Pie with Cheesy Mash

Fish pie is a real staple of Irish family cooking and everyone has their own way of making it. This is my version, which everyone always seems to enjoy. Don't use too much smoked cod or you will find the flavour to be too overpowering. Serves 6–8

350g (12oz) haddock, skin on and pin bones removed
350g (12oz) natural smoked cod, skin on and pin bones removed
350g (12oz) salmon fillets, skin on and pin bones removed
900ml (1 ½ pints) milk
1 large bay leaf
1.2kg (2lb 10oz) potatoes
150g (5oz) mature Cheddar cheese, grated
50g (2oz) butter, plus extra for greasing
225g (8oz) leeks, thinly sliced
1 small onion, thinly sliced
75g (3oz) plain flour
150ml (¼ pint) dry white wine
2 tbsp crème fraîche
1 tbsp chopped fresh flat-leaf parsley
200g (7oz) baby spinach
150g (5oz) cooked peeled prawns
2 heaped tbsp toasted breadcrumbs
sea salt and freshly ground white pepper
buttered peas, to serve

Preheat the oven to 200°C (400°F/gas mark 6). Butter a 2.4 litre (4 pint) ovenproof dish that's about 5cm (2in) deep.

Remove any stray pin bones from the haddock, smoked cod and salmon and season generously, then place in a shallow pan with the milk and bay leaf. Bring to the boil, then reduce to a simmer and poach for 6–8 minutes, or until the fish flakes easily when tested with a knife. Remove the fish from the pan and take off any remaining skin. Flake the flesh into large chunks, checking for bones that might have been overlooked. Strain the leftover milk into a jug until you have 600ml (1 pint) for the sauce. Discard the bay leaf.

Peel the potatoes and cut into even-sized pieces and then place in a large pan of salted water. Bring to the boil, then reduce to a simmer and cook for about 20 minutes, or until tender. Drain and return to the pan to dry out a little. Mash well and beat in the Cheddar and half of the butter. Season well.

Melt the remaining butter in a small pan and gently cook the leeks and onion for about 5 minutes. Stir in the flour and cook for 1 minute, stirring constantly. Pour in the white wine and reduce by half. Gradually pour in the reserved 600ml (1 pint) of poaching milk and simmer for 6–8 minutes, until you have a smooth, thick sauce, stirring occasionally. Reduce the heat, then add the crème fraîche and parsley and remove from the heat.

Blanch the spinach in a pan of boiling water, then drain and run under cold water before squeezing it really dry.

Scatter the chunks of fish into the bottom of the buttered ovenproof dish and arrange the prawns on top with small mounds of the spinach. Cover with the sauce and then with a layer of the cheesy mash, spreading it with a palette knife. Rough up the top with a fork and then sprinkle over the breadcrumbs. Place on a baking sheet and cook for 25–30 minutes, until the top is bubbling and golden brown.

To serve, divide the seafood pie with the cheesy mash among warmed serving plates and add some buttered peas to each one.

Salmon and Asparagus Wraps with Rocket Pesto

Farmed salmon has become much better quality over the years and in my opinion some of the best available comes from Ireland, where the sea is always freezing cold and for the most part is unpolluted, with strong tidal flows. Make sure your salmon fillets are all even-sized and about 2.5cm (1in) thick to ensure even cooking. They also work well on the barbecue and can be made up to 12 hours in advance, covered with clingfilm and chilled until needed – just don't add the squeeze of lemon juice until you're ready to cook them. Serves 4

12 asparagus spears, trimmed
4 x 175g (6oz) skinless organic salmon
   fillets
4 fresh dill sprigs
4 slices Parma ham
juice of ½ lemon
1 tbsp olive oil
25g (1oz) butter
lightly dressed mixed salad, to serve

Biarritz poatoes (page 151), to serve
lemon wedges, to garnish

Rocket pesto:
25g (1oz) pine nuts
50g (2oz) rocket leaves
25g (1oz) freshly grated Parmesan
100ml (3 ½fl oz) rapeseed oil
sea salt and freshly ground black pepper

Preheat the oven to 190°C (375°F/gas mark 5).

To make the rocket pesto, place the pine nuts in a baking tin and roast for a few minutes, until golden brown, keeping a close eye on them to make sure they don't burn. Leave to cool. Place the rocket in a food processor with the toasted pine nuts, Parmesan and oil. Season with salt and pepper and blitz to a smooth purée. Place in a smal bowl, cover with clingfilm and chill until ready to use (this can be made up to 4 days in advance).

Blanch the asparagus spears in a pan of boiling salted water for 1 minute. Drain and quickly refresh under cold running water, then tip into a bowl of ice-cold water to cool completely. Drain well and pat dry on kitchen paper.

Season each salmon fillet with pepper and arrange 3 asparagus spears, trimming them down as necessary, and a dill sprig on top of each fillet. Lightly wrap a slice of Parma ham around each bundle and place in a shallow non-metallic dish, then add a squeeze of lemon juice.

Heat the olive oil in a large ovenproof frying pan over a medium-high heat and add the butter. Once it stops foaming, add the salmon wraps presentation-side down and cook for 4–5 minutes all over to seal. Transfer to the oven and roast for another 8 minutes, until the salmon wraps are cooked through.

To serve, arrange the salmon wraps on warmed serving plates and spoon some of the rocket pesto to one side. Add some mixed salad to each plate and place the rest of the rocket pesto on the table. Have a separate dish of Biarritz potatoes and lemon wedges.

Fish and Chips with Chunky Pea Purée and Tartare Sauce

Not just a take-away, this dish can be made at home without too much effort. Fierce battles rage over how best to coat the fish, but I have to say that this particular way of coating the fish in breadcrumbs gives a lovely crisp result. Serves 4

vegetable oil, for deep-frying
8 Rooster potatoes, peeled
100g (4oz) plain flour
2 eggs, beaten
200g (7oz) fresh white breadcrumbs
1 tsp chopped fresh flat-leaf parsley
1 tsp sesame seeds
4 x 175g (6oz) firm white fillets, boned and skinned (such as haddock, hake or pollack)
sea salt and freshly ground black pepper

Chunky pea purée:
400g (14oz) frozen peas
2 tbsp crème fraîche
squeeze of lemon juice, plus wedges to garnish

Tartare sauce:
150g (5oz) mayonnaise
50g (2oz) gherkins, rinsed and finely chopped
50g (2oz) capers, rinsed and finely chopped
1 tsp chopped fresh dill
1 tsp chopped fresh chives
squeeze of lemon juice

Preheat the oven to 150°C (300°F/gas mark 2).

Heat the vegetable oil in a deep-fat fryer or a deep-sided pan, making sure it's only half full, until it reaches 160°C (325°F). Cut the potatoes into skinny chips and then place in a bowl of cold water (this helps to remove the starch). Drain and then dry them as much as possible in a clean tea towel before placing them in a wire basket (you may need to do this in 2 batches, depending on the size of your basket) and lowering them into the heated oil. Cook for 3–4 minutes, until cooked through but not coloured. Drain well on kitchen paper and set aside.

Increase the temperature of the oil to 190°C (375°F) and prepare the fish. Place the flour on a flat plate and season to taste. Put the beaten eggs and some seasoning in a shallow dish and mix the breadcrumbs with the parsley and sesame seeds in another separate dish.

Coat the fish in the flour, shaking off any excess, then dip into the beaten egg and finally coat in the breadcrumbs. Quickly place in the heated oil and cook for 5–6 minutes, until crisp and golden brown – the exact time will depend on the thickness of the fillets (again, you may have to do this in 2 batches). Drain on kitchen paper and keep warm in the oven – this should only be for 1–2 minutes, so the batter doesn't lose any of its crispness.

To make the chunky pea purée, cook the peas in a pan of boiling salted water for 2–3 minutes, until tender. Drain and return to the pan. Add the crème fraîche and lemon juice, then season to taste. Using a hand blender, blitz to a chunky purée. Keep warm.

To make the tartare sauce, mix the mayonnaise in a bowl with the gherkins, capers, herbs, lemon juice and seasoning.

To serve, tip the blanched chips back into the wire basket and then carefully lower into the heated oil. Cook for 1–2 minutes, until crisp and golden brown. Drain well on kitchen paper and season with salt, then arrange on warmed serving plates with the crispy fish, chunky pea purée, tartare sauce and lemon wedges.

Aromatic Steamed Sea Bass with Soya Bean Salad

The fresh, zingy flavour of the ginger complements the steamed sea bass perfectly. Just be careful not to overcook the fish – it should still be very moist and tender when it's served. Use whatever leaves are freshest and in season, but the mustard kick of the mizuna works particularly well here. Serves 4

4 x 150g (5oz) skinless, boneless sea bass fillets
2 garlic cloves, finely chopped
2 spring onions, finely chopped
2 tsp freshly grated root ginger
2 tsp toasted sesame oil
fresh coriander leaves, to garnish

Soya bean salad:
300g (11oz) frozen soya beans
1 bunch of red radishes, trimmed and thinly sliced
100g (4oz) mizuna or wild rocket leaves
4 tbsp mirin
2 tbsp fresh lemon juice
1 tbsp dark soy sauce
1 tsp dried chilli flakes

Set up a steamer or put a rack into a wok or deep-sided pan with a lid (a clear glass one is best so that you can keep an eye on the fish while it's cooking). Pour in enough water to come 5cm (2in) up the sides and bring to the boil.

Arrange the sea bass fillets on a heatproof plate lined with a large piece of parchment paper (you can use the excess to help you lift out the fish once it has cooked) and put it on the rack. Scatter over the garlic, spring onions and ginger and drizzle over the sesame oil. Cover tightly and steam for 6–8 minutes, depending on the thickness of the fillets. They should have turned opaque and be flaking slightly but still moist.

Meanwhile, make the salad. Place the soya beans in a pan of boiling salted water and cook for 2–3 minutes, or until tender. Drain and quickly refresh under cold running water, then toss with the radishes and mizuna or wild rocket. Combine the mirin, lemon juice, soy sauce and chilli flakes in a small bowl to make the dressing.

To serve, divide the soya bean salad between the serving plates and top each one with a piece of the aromatic sea bass. Drizzle over the dressing and scatter over the coriander leaves.

EGGS

Smoked Salmon and Leek Quiche

You can make the pastry case for this tart up to 24 hours in advance, but if you're short of time you can always use shop-bought pastry or even a ready-made pastry case instead. When I go to the trouble of making pastry I normally make double the quantity I need and freeze the rest to use another day. **Serves 6**

25g (1oz) butter
1 small leek, diced
150ml (¼ pint) cream
150ml (¼ pint) milk
2 eggs
2 egg yolks
2 tbsp sweet chilli sauce
1 tbsp chopped fresh flat-leaf parsley
1 tbsp chopped fresh dill
200g (7oz) smoked salmon, diced
sea salt and freshly ground black pepper
lightly dressed green salad, to serve

For the pastry:
225g (8oz) plain flour, extra for dusting
100g (4oz) butter, diced and chilled
½ tsp salt
good pinch of chilli powder (optional)
3 tbsp ice-cold water
1 egg yolk
1 tbsp milk

To make the pastry, place the flour, butter, salt and chilli powder (if using) in a food processor. Whizz briefly until the mixture forms fine crumbs. Pour in the water through the feeder tube and pulse again so that the pastry comes together. Knead gently on a lightly floured surface for a few seconds to form a smooth dough. Wrap in clingfilm and chill for at least 10 minutes before rolling (or up to 1 hour if time allows).

Roll out the pastry on a lightly floured surface and use to line a loose-bottomed 21cm (8 ½in) fluted flan tin that's about 4cm (1 ½in) deep. Use a rolling pin to lift the pastry into the tin, pressing well into the sides and letting the pastry overhang a little, as this prevents shrinkage. Chill for another 10 minutes for the pastry to rest.

Preheat the oven to 200°C (400°F/gas mark 6).

Prick the pastry base with a fork, then line with a circle of oiled foil or parchment paper that is first crumpled up to make it easier to handle. Fill with baking beans or dried pulses and bake for 20 minutes, until the pastry case looks 'set' but not coloured.

Beat the egg yolk and milk together in a small bowl. Carefully remove the foil or paper and lower the temperature to 160°C (325°F/gas mark 3), then brush the pastry with the egg wash to form a seal. Return to the oven for 5 minutes, or until the base is firm to the touch and the sides are lightly coloured. Remove the pastry from the oven, then increase the heat to 180°C (350°F/ gas mark 4).

While the pastry is baking, heat the butter in a frying pan over a medium heat and sauté the leek for 3–4 minutes, until it's softened but not coloured. Season to taste and leave to cool.

Beat the cream in a bowl with the milk, eggs, egg yolks and sweet chilli sauce, until well combined. Stir in the parsley and dill and season with salt and pepper. Scatter the leek and smoked salmon into the bottom of the pastry case and then pour in the cream mixture. Bake for 25–30 minutes, until the filling is just set but still slightly wobbly in the middle. Leave to rest for 5 minutes in the tin, then remove and trim down the excess pastry.

To serve, carefully cut the smoked salmon and leek quiche into slices while it's still warm. Arrange on serving plates with the green salad.

Variations

Caramelised Onion Quiche with Boilíe Goat's Cheese and Semi-sun-dried Tomatoes

Heat 1 tablespoon of olive oil in a heavy-based pan over a medium heat with a good knob of butter. Sweat 3 thinly sliced Spanish onions in the pan for about 30 minutes, until well reduced and nicely caramelised, stirring regularly to prevent them from sticking. Season to taste and stir in ½ teaspoon chopped fresh thyme. Leave to cool completely and then spread over the bottom of the pastry case. Scatter over 225g (8oz) Boilíe goat's cheese balls and 100g (4oz) chopped semi-sun-dried tomatoes. Replace the parsley and dill with chives and finish as described above.

Classic Quiche

Omit the chilli powder from the pastry. Heat a little oil in a frying pan over a medium heat and cook 175g (6oz) of diced rindless smoked bacon until crispy. Drain on kitchen paper and then spread over the bottom of the pastry case. Finish as described above but omit the smoked samon, leek, herbs and sweet chilli sauce.

Mushroom Omelette

Omelettes are so quick to make that it's just not worth cooking a large one for 2 people. Of course, you could put in any filling that you fancy, such as roasted peppers or crispy bacon and spring onions, depending on what's in the fridge. Serves 1

2 tsp sunflower oil
knob of unsalted butter
100g (4oz) chestnut mushrooms, sliced
3 large eggs
1 tsp snipped fresh chives
sea salt and freshly ground black pepper
lightly dressed rocket salad, to serve (optional)
crusty French bread, to serve (optional)

Heat a non-stick frying pan with a base that's about 20cm (8in) in diameter. Add 1 teaspoon of the oil and a little butter. Once the butter is foaming, tip in the mushrooms. Season to taste and then sauté for 2–3 minutes over a medium-high heat, until tender. Tip into a bowl and set aside.

Wipe out the frying pan and return to the hob over a medium heat. Break the eggs into a bowl and add the chives, then season and lightly beat. Don't be tempted to overbeat the eggs, as it will spoil the texture.

When the pan is hot, add the remaining teaspoon of oil and then the butter, swirling the pan around so that the base and sides get coated. While the butter is still foaming, pour in the eggs, tilting the pan from side to side. Stir gently with a fork or wooden spatula, drawing the mixture from the sides to the centre as it sets. When the eggs have almost set, scatter over the reserved mushrooms. Tilt the pan away from you slightly and use a palette knife to fold over the omelette.

To serve, slide the mushroom omelette onto a warmed serving plate and add the rocket salad and some crusty bread, if liked.

Huevos Rancheros

This recipe of baked eggs on a bed of spiced peppers and tomatoes is traditionally served in Mexico for breakfast. There are numerous versions from around the world, including one from Tunisia, which is called chakchouka and has no chilli. **Serves 4**

1 tbsp rapeseed oil
100g (4oz) chorizo, finely sliced (halved and quartered, if large)
2 garlic cloves, crushed
1 large onion, thinly sliced
1 red pepper, halved, seeded and thinly sliced
1 yellow pepper, halved, seeded and thinly sliced
1 red chilli, seeded and finely chopped
1 tsp caster sugar
½ tsp cumin seeds
400g (14oz) can chopped tomatoes
4 large eggs
sea salt and freshly ground black pepper
chopped fresh flat-leaf parsley, to garnish
ciabatta bread, to serve

Preheat the oven to 180°C (350°F/gas mark 4).

Heat the oil in a 28cm (11in) ovenproof frying pan over a medium heat and sauté the chorizo until it's sizzling. Transfer the chorizo to a plate with a slotted spoon, leaving behind the flavoured oil. Tip in the garlic, onion, peppers and chilli and fry over a medium heat for 8–10 minutes, until well softened but not coloured, stirring occasionally. Stir in the sugar and cumin seeds and then pour in the chopped tomatoes, stirring to combine. Bring to a simmer, then cook for 5 minutes, until the peppers are completely tender and the sauce has slightly reduced and thickened. Season to taste and fold the chorizo back in.

Using the back of a wooden spoon, make 4 holes in the pepper mixture that are just large enough to fit the eggs, then carefully crack an egg into each hole. Season and cook for 6–8 minutes, or until the whites of the eggs are set but the yolks are still runny.

Scatter over the parsley to garnish and serve straight from the frying pan to the table with plenty of ciabatta bread to mop up all the delicious sauce.

Smoked Bacon Frittata with Parmesan

It's important not to overbeat the eggs or the texture of this frittata will become tough. Serve it with some sliced flat mushrooms that have been sautéed in garlic butter to make this into a very special breakfast indeed. Serves 4

2 tbsp rapeseed oil
25g (1oz) unsalted butter
3 Spanish onions, thinly sliced
6 rindless smoked bacon rashers, cut into
    small lardons
2 garlic cloves, crushed
1 tsp fresh thyme leaves

8 large eggs, lightly beaten
50g (2oz) freshly grated Parmesan
1 tsp finely chopped fresh sage
1 tbsp chopped fresh flat-leaf parsley
lightly dressed salad leaves, to serve
sea salt and freshly ground black pepper

Heat 1 tablespoon of oil and all the butter in a large sauté or frying pan. Add the onions and start by cooking over a fairly high heat, stirring constantly until they begin to soften but not brown. Reduce the heat and continue to cook over a medium heat, stirring frequently so the onions don't stick or colour. They will need about 30 minutes in total to caramelise.

Stir the bacon into the onions with the garlic and thyme 5 minutes before the end of the cooking time and continue to cook until the bacon has begun to sizzle and crisp up. Tip into a large bowl and leave to cool.

Preheat the oven to 180°C (350°F/gas mark 4).

Add the eggs, Parmesan, sage and some salt and pepper to the onion and bacon mixture and stir well to combine.

Heat 1 tablespoon of oil in an ovenproof heavy-based pan that's about 20cm (8in) in diameter and deep enough to take the mixture. Swirl to coat the sides of the pan evenly with the oil, then pour in the egg mixture and cook for 6–8 minutes over a low heat to set the bottom and sides. Transfer the pan to the oven and cook, uncovered, for about 20 minutes, until just set, puffed up and lightly golden. Remove from the oven and leave to settle for 5 minutes.

To serve, scatter over the parsley, then loosen the sides with a palette knife and cut the frittata into wedges. Serve warm or cold onto serving plates, straight from the pan. Have a bowl of salad leaves on the table so that everyone can help themselves.

Eggs Benedict

This is my version of eggs Benedict, which is a poached egg served on a split muffin with crispy bacon and a warm butter sauce, which is much lighter than hollandaise. It's also fantastic served with smoked salmon, which is known as eggs royale, or slices of hand-carved cooked ham.
Serves 4

1 tbsp white wine vinegar
8 eggs
16 smoked streaky bacon rashers, rinds removed
4 English breakfast muffins, split in half
25g (1oz) unsalted butter, softened
fresh chervil sprigs, to garnish

Butter sauce:
100ml (3 ½fl oz) cream
1 tsp Dijon mustard
25g (1oz) butter, softened
1 tsp cornflour, sifted
squeeze of lemon juice
1 tsp snipped fresh chives
sea salt and freshly ground black pepper

Heat a large pan with 2.25 litres (4 pints) water. Add the white wine vinegar and bring to the boil. Break each egg into the water where it's bubbling, then reduce the heat and simmer gently for 3 minutes, until the eggs are just cooked through but the yolks are still soft. Remove with a slotted spoon and plunge into a bowl of iced water.

Preheat the grill, then grill the bacon until it's crispy and golden, turning regularly. Toast the muffins, cut side up, and spread with the butter.

Meanwhile, to make the butter sauce, place the cream and mustard in a small pan and simmer for 1 minute. Whisk in the butter, cornflour and lemon juice, then continue to whisk for 2–3 minutes, until thickened. Stir in the chives and season to taste. Keep warm.

Bring a large pan of salted water to the boil, then reduce to a simmer. Add the poached eggs and cook for 1 minute to warm through.

To serve, place 2 muffin halves on each warmed serving plate and put 2 slices of bacon on top of each one. Using a slotted spoon, remove the poached eggs from the pan and drain briefly on kitchen paper. Place an egg on the bacon and spoon over the butter sauce. Garnish with the chervil sprigs.

VEGETARIAN

Penne and Broad Bean Gratin

The broad beans add a wonderful zap to this pasta gratin, while the flavoured mascarpone cream helps to keep everything really moist. This dish can be prepared several hours in advance and just popped into a preheated oven at 180°C (350°F/gas mark 4) for 25–30 minutes or until heated through, and then flashed under the grill until bubbling. **Serves 4–6**

500g (1lb 2oz) fresh or frozen broad
  beans
350g (12oz) penne pasta
300ml (½ pint) dry white wine
300ml (½ pint) cream
250g (9oz) mascarpone cheese
75g (3oz) freshly grated Pecorino
25g (1oz) freshly grated Parmesan
2 egg yolks

2 tbsp snipped fresh chives
2 tbsp shredded fresh basil, extra leaves
  to garnish
250g (9oz) baby spinach
280g (10oz) jar of artichoke hearts,
  drained and halved
sea salt and freshly ground black pepper
lightly dressed rocket, to serve (optional)

Place the broad beans in a pan of boiling salted water and cook for 2–3 minutes (or about 5 minutes if frozen), or until just tender. Drain and refresh under cold running water, then slip the beans out of their skins.

Preheat the grill to medium. Plunge the penne into a large pan of boiling salted water and cook for 8–10 minutes, or according to the packet instructions, until al dente. Drain well.

Meanwhile, reduce the white wine in a wide pan over a high heat for about 10 minutes, until it has evaporated to about 2 tablespoons. Add the cream and bring to the boil, then season and reduce the heat. Simmer gently for 6–8 minutes, until slightly reduced and thickened. Leave to cool slightly.

Beat together the mascarpone cheese, most of the Pecorino (reserve a handful to sprinkle on top of the gratin), the Parmesan, egg yolks, chives and basil in a bowl.

Stir the broad beans into the cooked penne along with the baby spinach until it's wilted, then stir in the artichoke hearts and the cream mixture and tip into a shallow ovenproof dish about 23cm (9in) square and 5cm (2in) deep.

Spoon dollops of the mascarpone cheese mixture over the penne and spread using a palette knife or the back of the spoon until the penne is completely covered, then scatter over the reserved Pecorino. Place under the grill and cook for about 5 minutes, until bubbling and lightly golden.

To serve, place the penne and broad bean gratin straight on the table. Garnish with the basil leaves and divide among warmed serving plates with the rocket salad, if liked.

Roasted Root Vegetables with Buttermilk Dressing and Coriander Couscous

This dish is delicious hot or cold. Try using any combination of root vegetables you fancy. However, it's important that the vegetables aren't too crowded in the roasting tin, otherwise they'll stew rather than roast. If in doubt, use 2 smaller tins and swap the shelves in the oven halfway through roasting to ensure they cook evenly. Serves 4

20 baby carrots, peeled and trimmed
12 baby beetroot, trimmed and halved
10 baby leeks, trimmed and halved
4 tbsp balsamic vinegar
2 tbsp caster sugar
5 tbsp extra virgin olive oil
225g (8oz) couscous
juice of ½ lemon

2 tbsp chopped fresh coriander
sea salt and freshly ground black pepper
lightly dressed salad, to serve

Buttermilk dressing:
75g (3oz) soft goat's cheese or curd
75ml (3fl oz) buttermilk

Preheat the oven to 200°C (400°F/gas mark 6). Line a large roasting tin with parchment paper.

Place the carrots, beetroot and leeks in a bowl with the balsamic vinegar, sugar and 2 table-spoons of olive oil, then toss to combine. Tip into the lined tin and roast for 20–25 minutes, or until the vegetables are just soft.

To make the buttermilk dressing, whisk the goat's cheese and buttermilk until smooth and season to taste.

Five minutes before the end of the vegetables' cooking time, place the couscous in a large pan and drizzle over the remaining 3 tablespoons of olive oil along with the lemon juice, stirring gently to combine. Pour over 225ml (8fl oz) of boiling water, then stir well, cover and leave to stand for 5 minutes before gently separating the grains with a fork. Season to taste and then reheat gently, stirring continuously with a fork. Remove from the heat and stir in the coriander.

To serve, arrange the coriander couscous on warmed serving plates with the roasted root vegetables and drizzle around the buttermilk dressing. Garnish with a good grinding of black pepper and the salad.

Roast Pumpkin Risotto with Rocket Pesto

If you don't have a mini blender or liquidiser to make the rocket pesto, just finely chop the rocket using a large sharp knife and stir in the Parmesan and olive oil until combined.
Serves 4

1 small pumpkin about 800g (1lb 13oz),
  peeled, seeded and cut into small dice
4 tbsp olive oil
1.5 litres (2 ½ pints) vegetable stock (page 225)
75g (3oz) unsalted butter
2 garlic cloves, crushed
1 small onion, thinly sliced
2 tsp chopped fresh sage
350g (12oz) Arborio rice (risotto)
150ml (¼ pint) dry white wine
1 tbsp roughly chopped fresh flat-leaf parsley

Rocket pesto:
50ml (2fl oz) rapeseed oil
25g (1oz) rocket
1 small garlic clove, roughly chopped
2 tbsp freshly grated Parmesan
1 ½ tbsp toasted pine nuts
sea salt and freshly ground black pepper

Preheat the oven to 200°C (400°F/gas mark 6).

Scatter the pumpkin cubes into a large roasting tin and drizzle over 2 tablespoons of olive oil. Roast for 15–20 minutes, or until tender.

To make the rocket pesto, place the rapeseed oil in a mini blender or liquidiser with the rocket, garlic, Parmesan and pine nuts. Blend briefly to combine – it should retain some texture; you don't want it to be too smooth. Season to taste, transfer to a bowl and cover with clingfilm, then chill until ready to use.

Pour the stock into a pan and bring up to a gentle simmer. Heat the remaining 2 tablespoons of oil and 50g (2oz) of the butter in a separate large pan. Add the garlic, onion and sage and cook over a medium heat for 4–5 minutes, until softened but not coloured, stirring occasionally.

Increase the heat and add the rice, then cook for 1 minute, stirring continuously, until all of the grains are evenly coated and the rice is opaque. Pour in the wine and cook for 1–2 minutes, stirring. Reduce the heat to medium and add a ladleful of warm stock. Allow it to reduce down, stirring until it's completely absorbed. Continue to add the simmering stock a ladleful at a time, stirring frequently. Allow each ladleful of stock to be almost completely absorbed before adding the next ladleful until the rice is al dente – just tender but with a slight bite; this should take 20–25 minutes.

To serve, stir in the remaining 25g (1oz) of butter and the parsley. Carefully fold in the roasted pumpkin, season to taste and divide among warmed wide-rimmed serving bowls. Drizzle each one with a little of the rocket pesto (any remaining pesto can be served separately in a small bowl) and garnish with the reserved Parmesan.

Variations

Mixed Mushroom
Soak 25g (1oz) of dried cep or porcini mushrooms in 150ml (¼ pint) of warm water for 15 minutes. Pour the mushroom soaking liquid into the rice instead of wine. Chop the dried mushrooms and add them too. Slice 350g (12oz) mixed fresh mushrooms and sauté them in a knob of butter and 1 tablespoon of oil for 3–4 minutes. Fold into the risotto with a squeeze of lemon juice, chopped flat-leaf parsley and the Parmesan cheese.

Barley and Pea
Replace the rice with barley and stir in 175g (6oz) of fresh or frozen peas for the last 3–4 minutes of the cooking time. Add chopped fresh parsley and season generously with black pepper to serve.

Sweet Potato Cakes with Chilli and Feta

This makes a delicious lunch or light supper with very little effort. The sweet potato cakes are packed full of flavour, but it's a recipe that the whole family should enjoy. It's worth pressing the sweet potato cakes down gently with a palette knife or fish slice as they cook to help them keep their shape. Serves 4

450g (1lb) sweet potatoes
5 spring onions, finely chopped
1 red chilli, seeded and finely chopped
100g (4oz) feta cheese
2 large eggs
4 tbsp milk
50g (2oz) self-raising flour
25g (1oz) cornflour
vegetable oil, for cooking
sea salt and freshly ground black pepper

Cucumber raita:
1 small cucumber
150g (5oz) natural yoghurt
1 small garlic clove, crushed
1 tbsp finely chopped fresh flat-leaf parsley
1 tbsp finely chopped fresh mint

Salad:
100g (4oz) rocket
12 cherry tomatoes, halved
1 ripe Hass avocado, halved, peeled and cut into chunks
handful of pitted black olives (preserved in oil and drained)
1 tbsp extra virgin olive oil
1 tsp balsamic vinegar

Preheat the oven to 100°C (200°F/gas mark ¼).

Peel and grate the sweet potatoes – you'll need 350g (12oz) in total – and place in a bowl with the spring onions and chilli. Crumble in the feta and season. Break the eggs into a jug and beat with the milk. Sift the self-raising flour and the cornflour over the sweet potato mixture and then mix in the eggs and milk until you have a thick batter.

Heat about 2 tablespoons of oil in a large non-stick frying pan on a low heat. Working in batches, add in large spoonfuls of the sweet potato mixture, pressing them down with the back of a spoon until they're about 1cm (½in) thick. Cook gently for 3–4 minutes on each side, until golden brown, carefully turning them over with a fish slice to avoid breaking them up. Keep warm in a low oven while you cook the rest, adding more oil to the pan between batches if needed.

To make the cucumber raita, cut the cucumber into quarters and remove the seeds, then grate, squeezing out all the excess moisture. Mix into the yoghurt with the garlic and herbs, then season to taste.

To make the salad, place the rocket in a bowl with the tomatoes, avocado and olives. Lightly dress with the olive oil and balsamic vinegar. Season to taste.

To serve, arrange the sweet potato cakes on serving plates with a dollop of the cucumber raita. Have a separate dish of the dressed salad to hand around separately.

Spicy Chickpea and Sweet Potato Curry

Vegetarian dishes form a large part of the southern Indian diet, especially in the city of Madras. This curry is a worthy partner to basmati rice or naan bread, but goes equally well with grilled or roasted spicy-flavoured meats if you aren't a vegetarian. Serves 4

2 tbsp vegetable oil
450g (1lb) sweet potatoes, peeled and cut into 2cm (½in) slices
1 small onion, thinly sliced
2 garlic cloves, crushed
1 green chilli, seeded and finely chopped
1 tsp finely chopped fresh root ginger
1 tsp garam masala
1 tsp mild chilli powder
1 tsp ground turmeric

400g (14oz) can chopped tomatoes
300ml (½ pint) vegetable stock (page 225)
400g (14oz) can chickpeas, drained and rinsed
175g (6oz) spinach
sea salt and freshly ground black pepper
1 tbsp chopped fresh coriander, to garnish
steamed basmati rice, to serve

Heat the oil in a large pan and add the sweet potatoes. Cook for 2–3 minutes over a medium heat, turning once, until just beginning to colour (you may have to do this in batches depending on the size of your pan). Remove from the pan with a slotted spoon and place in a bowl. Add the onion to the oil left in the pan and sauté for 2–3 minutes, until softened, then add the garlic, chilli and ginger and cook for 1–2 minutes, stirring.

Add the garam masala to the pan with the chilli powder and ground turmeric and cook for another minute, stirring continuously. Stir in the tomatoes and bring to a gentle simmer. Cook for 15–20 minutes, until well reduced and thickened, stirring occasionally to prevent the bottom from sticking.

Pour the stock into the pan and then add the chickpeas and reserved sweet potato slices, stirring to combine. Simmer gently for another 30 minutes, or until the liquid has reduced to a sauce consistency.

Wash the spinach and remove any tough stalks, then once the sauce has achieved the correct consistency, add to the pan and allow to just wilt down. Season to taste.

To serve, spoon the chickpea and sweet potato curry into warmed serving bowls and garnish with the coriander. Place a separate bowl of rice on the table and allow people to help themselves.

TAKE-
AWAY MY
WAY

Neapolitan Pizza

The classic, original pizza – nothing else comes near it in terms of simplicity and balance. These pizzas are incredibly easy to make using sachets of easy-blend yeast and only need to be left to rise and prove once. These pizzas (see the variations on page 114 too) are a fantastic vehicle for all sorts of toppings, but don't be tempted to overload them or the base will become soggy. **Serves 4**

350g (12oz) strong white flour, extra for dusting
7g sachet easy-blend yeast
1 tsp salt
225ml (8fl oz) warm water
2 tbsp extra virgin olive oil, extra for greasing and drizzling
2 tsp semolina or dried white breadcrumbs
8 tbsp passata rustica (crushed tomatoes)
a few fresh basil leaves, torn, extra to garnish
150g (5oz) ball of mozzarella, drained and roughly chopped
25g (1oz) freshly grated Parmesan
40g (1½oz) rocket
sea salt and freshly ground black pepper

Place the flour, yeast and salt in a food processor fitted with a dough attachment (or use a bowl and a wooden spoon if you don't have a processor). Mix the warm water and oil in a jug. With the motor running, slowly pour the oil mixture through the feeder tube (or stir by hand) and mix until you have achieved a soft, stretchy dough. Knead for 5 minutes in the machine or for 10 minutes by hand on a lightly floured work surface.

Transfer the dough to a lightly oiled bowl. Rub the top with a little more oil and then cover with a clean, damp tea towel. Set aside at room temperature for 1 hour, or until the dough has doubled in size.

Preheat the oven to 240°C (475°F/gas mark 9).

Punch the dough down with a clenched fist. Remove the dough from the bowl and knead for a couple of minutes until smooth, then cut in half and roll each half out on a lightly floured surface into a 25cm (10in) circle. Sprinkle the semolina or breadcrumbs onto 2 large, flat baking sheets and transfer the pizza bases on top.

Season the passata to taste and then spread it over the pizza bases, leaving a 1cm (½in) border around the edges. Scatter over the basil, then drizzle over a little olive oil and scatter the mozzarella and Parmesan on top. Bake for 10–12 minutes, until the base is crisp and the cheeses are bubbling and lightly golden. Remove from the oven and drizzle over a little more olive oil, then scatter over the rocket and garnish with more basil. Season to taste.

To serve, cut the pizzas into wedges and arrange on warmed serving plates.

Variations

American Hot

Prepare the bases with the passata, basil and olive oil and then scatter over 50g (2oz) thinly sliced pepperoni and 50g (2oz) drained, sliced jalapeño chillies (from a jar or can). Finish and serve as described above.

Caramelised Onion and Goat's Cheese

Sauté 3 thinly sliced large onions in a little rapeseed oil for 30 minutes to 1 hour, until well caramelised, stirring regularly. Spread the onions over the pizza bases and then sprinkle over ¼ teaspoon of chopped fresh rosemary and dot with 100–175g (4–6oz) goat's cheese cubes. Cook and finish as described above.

Indian Lamb Bhuna

I like to serve this with some pilau rice with a dollop of mango chutney and plenty of warm naan. This is a roasted, relatively dry curry that tastes even better when it has been made a couple of days beforehand, giving the spices a chance to penetrate the meat and giving the lamb a chance to become even more tender. Serves 4–6

3 tbsp rapeseed oil
675g (1 ½lb) lamb neck fillet, cut into bite-sized pieces
6 whole cloves
2 bay leaves
1 small cinnamon stick
1 large onion, thinly sliced
4 garlic cloves, crushed
5cm (2in) piece of fresh root ginger, peeled and finely grated
1 tbsp ground coriander
2 tsp ground cumin
1 ½ tsp paprika
1 tsp cayenne pepper
¼ tsp ground cardamom
250ml (9fl oz) carton coconut cream
400g (14oz) can plum tomatoes, drained and finely chopped
sea salt and freshly ground black pepper
pilau rice, to serve
warm naan bread, to serve
mango chutney, to serve

Preheat the oven to 160°C (325°F/gas mark 3).

Heat 2 tablespoons of oil in a large ovenproof casserole with a lid. Add half of the lamb and fry over a medium heat until nicely browned all over. Transfer to a plate and fry the rest of the meat. Set aside.

Add the remaining tablespoon of oil to the pan and fry the cloves, bay leaves and cinnamon stick for a few seconds. Add the onion and fry for 6–7 minutes, until nicely browned. Add the garlic and ginger and fry for 2 minutes, then add the ground spices and fry for 1 minute more. Add the coconut cream a tablespoon at a time, frying for about 30 seconds between each addition.

Return the lamb to the pan and stir in the chopped tomatoes. Season to taste, cover with the lid and place in the oven for 1 hour, or until the lamb is meltingly tender but still holding its shape.

To serve, spoon the lamb bhuna onto warmed serving plates with the pilau rice. Have warm naan breads and mango chutney to hand around separately.

Thai Green Prawn Curry

Thai curries are very quick and easy to prepare, especially now that most supermarkets sell authentic ready-made curry pastes. If you're really keen I suppose you could always make your own, but I never usually bother. I like to serve mine with Thai fragrant rice. The long white grains have a characteristically soft and slightly sticky texture when cooked. Serves 4

50g (2oz) bunch of fresh coriander
4 shallots, chopped
2 garlic cloves, chopped
2 tbsp rapeseed oil
2 tbsp Thai green curry paste
2 x 400g (14oz) cans coconut milk
225ml (8fl oz) chicken stock (page 226)
175g (6oz) baby new potatoes, halved
2 tbsp Thai fish sauce (nam pla) or light soy sauce
finely grated rind and juice of 1 lime
1 tbsp caster sugar
450g (1lb) peeled raw tiger prawns (tails intact)
100g (4oz) cherry tomatoes, halved
sea salt and freshly ground black pepper
Thai fragrant rice, to serve
good handful of fresh basil leaves, roughly torn, to serve
lime wedges, to serve

Remove about a quarter of the coriander leaves from the stalks and reserve. Roughly chop the remainder, including the stalks, and place in a mini blender with the shallots and garlic. Whizz to a paste.

Heat a wok or heavy-based frying pan. Add the oil and stir-fry the green curry paste for 1 minute over a high heat. Add 150ml (¼ pint) of the coconut milk and the coriander paste, stirring well to combine. Cook for 2 minutes, then add the chicken stock and boil for 8–10 minutes, or until the natural oils start to appear on the surface, stirring occasionally. Season generously.

Stir in the potatoes, reduce the heat and simmer for 15 minutes, or until the potatoes are completely tender and the sauce has reduced considerably, with the oils clearly visible on the surface.

Add the remaining coconut milk, the fish sauce or soy sauce, lime rind and juice and sugar. Bring to a simmer and then tip in the prawns and cherry tomatoes. Cook for another 2–3 minutes, until the prawns are just tender. Add the reserved coriander leaves and cook for another minute, stirring. To serve, place the rice in warmed serving bowls and spoon over the Thai green prawn curry. Scatter over the basil to garnish and have lime wedges on the table in a separate dish.

Variations

Thai Yellow Chicken Curry

Replace the green curry paste with yellow. Add 12 boneless, skinless chicken thighs that have been cut into bite-sized pieces instead of the prawns and simmer for 15 minutes, until tender.

Thai Red Duck Curry

Replace the green curry paste with red. Add 675g (1 ½lb) Peking duck breasts, skin removed and cut into bite-sized pieces, instead of the prawns and simmer for 15 minutes, until tender. Finish with the coriander leaves before serving.

Sizzling Steak Fajitas with Tomato Salsa and Guacamole

This is a great dish that all of the family should enjoy and is perfect to put in the centre of the table so that everyone can dig in. The beef can be marinated well in advance, leaving very little to do last minute. **Serves 4**

2 garlic cloves, crushed
finely grated rind and juice of 1 lime
1 tsp ground cumin
½ tsp ground coriander
good pinch of paprika
3 tbsp olive oil
450g (1lb) beef striploin or sirloin, trimmed and cut into strips
1 large onion, thinly sliced
1 red pepper, seeded and cut into thin strips
1 yellow pepper, seeded and cut into thin strips
8 soft flour tortillas
sea salt and freshly ground black pepper
fresh coriander leaves, to garnish
6 tbsp sour cream, to serve

Tomato salsa:
2 spring onions, finely chopped
1 large ripe tomato, diced
1 mild red chilli, seeded and finely chopped

Guacamole:
2 ripe Hass avocados
juice of 1 lime

Place the garlic in a non-metallic dish with the lime rind and juice, cumin, coriander and paprika. Stir in 1 ½ tablespoons of olive oil. Add in the beef strips, cover with clingfilm and marinate for up to 2 hours, or overnight is best.

To make the salsa, place the spring onions, tomato and chilli in a bowl and mix well to combine. Season lightly and set aside at room temperature to allow the flavours to combine.

To make the guacamole, cut the avocados in half and remove the stones. Scoop out the flesh and roughly mash with a fork. Stir in the lime juice and season to taste.

To make the fajitas, heat the remaining 1 ½ tablespoons of olive oil in a large frying pan over a low heat and gently fry the onion and peppers for 6–8 minutes, until softened, stirring occasionally. Remove with a slotted spoon to a bowl and keep warm.

Raise the heat to high and add the marinated beef mixture and sauté for 4–5 minutes, until cooked through and lightly golden. Return the onion and peppers to the pan and stir-fry for another 2–3 minutes, until well combined and heated through. Season to taste.

Heat a frying or griddle pan. Add a soft flour tortilla and heat for 30 seconds, turning once, until soft and pliable. Repeat with the remaining tortillas and stack them up on a warmed plate.

To serve, transfer the sizzling beef mixture into a warmed serving bowl or platter and garnish with the fresh coriander. Hand around the warmed tortillas, tomato salsa, guacamole and sour cream, allowing each person to assemble the fajitas themselves.

Chicken Tikka Masala

This has to be the most popular curry in the world! There is always a debate about the exact origins of the recipe, but it's certainly not an authentic Indian curry and is most likely a result of the curry devised for Western palates in the first Indian restaurants in Britain and Ireland.
Serves 4

1 tbsp rapeseed oil
knob of butter
2 onions, thinly sliced
2 garlic cloves, crushed
1 red chilli, seeded and finely chopped
5cm (2in) piece of fresh root ginger,
  peeled and finely grated
100g (4oz) tikka masala curry paste (such
  as Patak's)
200g (7oz) canned chopped tomatoes
250ml (9fl oz) carton of coconut cream
150ml (¼ pint) chicken stock (page 226)
  or water

12 boneless, skinless chicken thighs or 4
  skinless chicken breast fillets, cut into
  thick strips
sea salt and freshly ground black pepper
200g (7oz) natural yoghurt, extra to
  garnish
fresh coriander leaves, to garnish

Saffron rice:
1 tsp saffron threads
knob of butter
350g (12oz) basmati rice
6 green cardamom pods, cracked

Heat the oil and butter in a large heavy-based pan with a lid. Add the onions, garlic, chilli and ginger and cook for 10 minutes over a medium heat, until soft and lightly golden. Stir in the tikka masala paste and cook for 1 minute. Season to taste. Add the tomatoes, coconut cream and chicken stock or water. Bring to the boil, then lower the heat and simmer for 15–20 minutes, until reduced by half and thickened.

Tip in the chicken strips and yoghurt and stir well to combine. Bring back to a gentle simmer, then cover with a lid and cook for another 15–20 minutes, until the sauce is nicely reduced and the chicken is tender.

To prepare the saffron rice, place the saffron threads into a small bowl and pour over a little boiling water and leave to infuse. Melt the butter in a large heavy-based pan with a lid. When it's just starting to foam, tip in the rice and cardamom. Stir the rice for 2 minutes over a medium heat and season with a little salt. Pour over enough boiling water to cover the rice by 2.5cm (1in), bring to a simmer and put on the lid. Allow to cook for 5 minutes, then pour in the saffron, including the water that it's been soaking in. Cover the pot again and continue to cook for a further 5 minutes, or until the rice is just cooked but retains some bite.

To serve, spoon the chicken tikka masala into warmed serving bowls and put the saffron rice into separate bowls. Add dollops of yoghurt to each bowl of chicken tikka masala and a good scattering of coriander leaves to garnish.

PASTA

Classic Italian Lasagne

To make spaghetti Bolognese, simply stir this meat sauce into spaghetti and sprinkle with freshly grated Parmesan to serve. This lasagne can be assembled ahead of time. I find the day before is best, as it gives time for the whole thing to settle and helps to create a firmer portion coming out of the dish when serving. It also freezes very well before it has been cooked and will keep for a couple of months well covered with clingfilm. Defrost thoroughly before baking. Serves 8

2 tbsp olive oil
2 garlic cloves, finely chopped
1 large onion, finely chopped
1 large carrot, finely diced
100g (4oz) button mushrooms, quartered
1 tsp chopped fresh thyme
675g (1 ½lb) lean minced beef
2 tbsp tomato purée
2 x 400g (14oz) cans chopped tomatoes
6 tinned anchovies, drained and finely chopped (optional)
2 tbsp dark soy sauce
1 tbsp shredded fresh basil, extra leaves to garnish
1 tbsp balsamic vinegar
1 tbsp caster sugar
9 dried lasagne sheets
50g (2oz) freshly grated Parmesan
sea salt and freshly ground black pepper
lightly dressed green salad, to serve
garlic bread, to serve

Cheese sauce:
1 small onion
6 whole cloves
750ml (1 pint 9fl oz) milk
1 bay leaf
50g (2oz) butter
50g (2oz) plain flour
150g (5oz) Cheddar cheese, grated

To make the Bolognese sauce, heat the oil in a large pan over a medium heat. Add the garlic, onion, carrot, mushrooms and thyme. Cook for 8–10 minutes, until the vegetables have softened and taken on a little colour, stirring occasionally. Add the minced beef and mix until well combined, then sauté until well browned, breaking up any lumps with a wooden spoon. Add in the tomato purée and continue to cook for another 1–2 minutes, stirring. Pour in the chopped tomatoes and add the anchovies (if using), soy sauce, basil, balsamic vinegar and sugar, then season to taste. Bring to the boil, then reduce the heat to the lowest setting and simmer for at least 1 hour, or up to 2 hours is fine, until the beef is meltingly tender and the sauce has reduced.

To make the cheese sauce, peel the onion and stud with the cloves, then place in a pan with the milk and bay leaf. Bring to a simmer, then remove from the heat and set aside to allow the flavours to infuse for at least 10 minutes, but up to 30 minutes is perfect. Strain and discard the studded onion and bay leaf.

Melt the butter in a pan over a medium heat. Add in the flour and cook for 1 minute, stirring. Remove from the heat and gradually pour in the infused milk, whisking until smooth after each addition. Season to taste. Bring the sauce to the boil, whisking constantly, then reduce the heat and simmer gently for 5 minutes, until smooth and thickened, stirring occasionally. Remove from the heat and stir in the Cheddar until melted.

To cook the lasagne, preheat the oven to 180°C (350°F/gas mark 4).

Line a 2.75 litre (5 pint) ovenproof dish that is 5cm (2in) deep with 3 lasagne sheets, breaking them to fit as necessary. Add half of the Bolognese and spread it into an even layer. Spread over a third of the cheese sauce. Cover with another 3 lasagne sheets. Use the rest of the Bolognese sauce to make another layer and then pour over another third of the cheese sauce. Cover with the remaining 3 lasagne sheets and spread the rest of the cheese sauce on top. Scatter over the Parmesan and bake for 45 minutes to 1 hour, until the lasagne is bubbling and lightly golden.

Serve the lasagne straight to the table garnished with the basil leaves, then cut into portions and arrange on warmed plates. Have a separate bowl of salad and a plate of garlic bread.

Classic Tomato Spaghetti

This pasta sauce literally takes the same time to make as the pasta does to cook, which means you can get dinner on the table in less than 15 minutes. Buy the best canned Italian plum tomatoes that you can find – as a rule, the more expensive they are, the better they are! They are the key ingredient to this simple pasta sauce and the thing that can transform it from a rustic dish to something much more special. Once you have mastered the basics you can add other simple ingredients to the sauce that will make it into a completely different meal (see the variations on page 129). Serves 4

400g (14oz) dried spaghetti
2 tbsp olive oil, extra for drizzling
2 garlic cloves, crushed
1 onion, finely chopped
400g (14oz) can Italian plum tomatoes (see note above)
pinch of sugar
sea salt and freshly ground black pepper
large handful of fresh basil leaves (optional)
Parmesan shavings, to serve

Bring a large pan of salted water to the boil. Add the spaghetti and cook for 8–10 minutes, or according to the instructions on the packet.

Meanwhile, heat the olive oil in a pan over a medium heat. Add the garlic and onion and cook for 2–3 minutes, until softened but not coloured. Tip in the tomatoes and sugar and season to taste, then mash with a potato masher to break down the tomatoes. Reduce the heat and simmer gently for 5–6 minutes, until the sauce has nicely reduced and thickened slightly. Blitz with a hand blender for a smooth sauce and season to taste.

Drain the spaghetti and return it to the pan, then stir in the tomato sauce until nicely combined.

To serve, divide the tomato spaghetti among warmed serving bowls and scatter over the basil, if using. Drizzle a little olive oil over each one and sprinkle over the Parmesan shavings.

Variations

Arrabiata

Add 1 finely chopped mild red chilli or ½ teaspoon of crushed chilli flakes in with the onion and garlic. Fold 2 teaspoons of roughly chopped fresh flat-leaf parsley into the spaghetti with the tomato sauce. If you like, garnish with the Parmesan as described above.

Vodka Cream

Use a short dried pasta such as farfalle, penne or fusilli. Add 4 tablespoons of cream once the sauce has been blended and simmer for another 1–2 minutes. Fold the sauce into the pasta with the basil, add a small glass of vodka and toss again. Do this off the heat – if the vodka evaporates, you will lose the taste. Garnish with freshly grated Parmesan as described above.

Puttanesca

Increase the garlic to 2 large cloves and add in 1 finely chopped mild red chilli or ½ teaspoon of crushed chilli flakes and 4 finely chopped anchovies, if liked. Fold into the spaghetti with 100g (4oz) of pitted black olives and 3 tablespoons of rinsed capers, then garnish with a little chopped fresh flat-leaf parsley.

Meatball Pasta Bake with Spinach and Mozzarella

All children seem to just love meatballs, and this pasta bake tastes particularly delicious. It's great if you want to feed a crowd, with nothing to do at the last minute except put together a quick salad. Just remember that if cooking from the fridge cold, give it an extra 10 minutes in the oven. Serves 4–6

225g (8oz) lean minced beef
225g (8oz) minced pork
8 cream crackers, crushed into fine crumbs
1 egg, lightly beaten
1 tbsp chopped fresh flat-leaf parsley
2 tbsp olive oil, extra for drizzling
1 onion, finely chopped
1 celery stick, finely chopped
1 large garlic clove, crushed
500ml (18fl oz) passata (Italian sieved tomatoes)
2 tbsp tomato purée
small handful of fresh basil leaves, extra to garnish
350g (12oz) penne pasta
knob of butter
225g (8oz) baby spinach leaves
100g (4oz) mozzarella, cut into cubes
25g (1oz) freshly grated Parmesan
sea salt and freshly ground black pepper
lightly dressed mixed salad, to serve

Place the minced beef and pork in a bowl with the crushed cream crackers, egg and parsley. Season with salt and pepper and using your hands, give everything a good mix. Using slightly wetted hands, make about 20 even-sized balls. Arrange on a flat baking sheet, drizzle over a little olive oil to lightly coat and chill for 1 hour to firm up if time allows.

Heat 1 tablespoon of olive oil in a large pan over a medium heat and sauté the onion and celery for about 5 minutes, until lightly golden. Add in the garlic and cook for 1 minute more, stirring. Add the passata and tomato purée and season to taste. Simmer gently for 8–10 minutes, until the sauce has nicely reduced and thickened. Stir in the basil leaves and remove from the heat.

Meanwhile, preheat the oven to 200°C (400°F/gas mark 6). Bring a large pot of salted water to the boil.

Plunge the penne into the boiling salted water and simmer for 6–8 minutes, until almost tender but not quite cooked through. Drain the penne well and return to the pan.

Heat the remaining 1 tablespoon of olive oil in a deep-sided frying pan over a medium heat and sauté the meatballs for 6–8 minutes, until almost cooked through and nicely browned.

Heat the butter in a separate pan. Add one fistful of spinach at a time, adding another as one wilts down. Cook for 1 minute, then tip into a colander to drain. Season to taste.

Stir the tomato sauce into the drained penne to coat and then transfer to a 30cm x 20cm (12in x 8in) 5cm (2in) deep ovenproof baking dish. Nestle in small mounds of spinach and arrange the meatballs on top. Scatter over the mozzarella and Parmesan. Place in the oven and bake for 15–20 minutes, until bubbling.

To serve, put the pasta bake straight on the table garnished with the basil leaves. Have a separate big bowl of salad and allow everyone to help themselves.

Roasted Butternut Squash and Pine Nut Pasta with Sage

This is the kind of pasta dish I tend to make when there's nothing much left in the fridge. It's very easy to prepare, and great served with a light rocket salad and a glass of decent wine. If you haven't got any mascarpone cheese, simply replace with a simple béchamel sauce. Serves 4

675g (1 ½lb) butternut squash
25g (1oz) butter
2 tbsp olive oil
1 tbsp chopped fresh sage
100g (4oz) rindless pancetta, cut into lardons
2 garlic cloves, crushed
1 red onion, finely diced
250g (9oz) mascarpone cheese
50g (2oz) freshly grated Parmesan
100ml (3 ½fl oz) vegetable stock (page 225)
275g (10oz) penne pasta
50g (2oz) toasted pine nuts
1 tsp chopped fresh basil
sea salt and freshly ground black pepper
lightly dressed green salad, to serve

Preheat the oven to 200°C (400°F/gas mark 6).

Peel the butternut squash, then cut in half. Scoop out and discard the seeds. Place the butter and 1 tablespoon of olive oil in a roasting tin. Place the tin in the oven for a few minutes to heat up. Cut the butternut squash into bite-sized chunks and then toss them into the heated tin. Add the sage and some salt and pepper and roast for 20 minutes, or until just cooked through. Keep warm.

Heat the remaining 1 tablespoon of olive oil in a frying pan over a medium heat and sauté the pancetta for 2–3 minutes, until sizzling. Add the garlic and onion and cook for 3–4 minutes, until the onion is softened and just beginning to brown and the pancetta is golden, stirring regularly. Stir in the mascarpone cheese, Parmesan and stock and simmer very gently for 4–5 minutes, until slightly reduced and thickened. Season to taste.

Meanwhile, cook the penne in a large pan of boiling salted water for 8–10 minutes, until al dente, or according to the packet instructions. Drain and then quickly refresh under cold running water. Return to the pan and stir in the mascarpone sauce, then carefully fold in the roasted butternut squash, pine nuts and chopped basil.

To serve, divide among warmed serving bowls and serve with a separate bowl of the salad.

Variations

Mushroom
Instead of the butternut squash, use 225g (8oz) sliced chestnut mushrooms and sauté them with the garlic and onion.

Ham and Pea
Add 100g (4oz) frozen petit pois or peas and 225g (8oz) chopped cooked ham to the mascarpone sauce with the pine nuts.

Chicken and Spinach
Add 175g (6oz) frozen leaf spinach to the mascarpone sauce with 225g (8oz) chopped cooked chicken.

Pasta Carbonara

This carbonara can be made with pastas other than spaghetti. You might try penne, linguini or tagliatelle, and they will all have the cooking instructions on the packet. It's a good, tasty recipe that takes very little effort and that most people seem to enjoy. Serves 4

350g (12oz) dried spaghetti
15g (½oz) butter
1 onion, finely chopped
1 garlic clove, crushed
225g (8oz) rindless pancetta or bacon rashers, cut into lardons
100ml (3 ½fl oz) dry white wine
3 eggs
50g (2oz) freshly grated Parmesan, extra to garnish
150ml (¼ pint) cream
1 tbsp chopped fresh flat-leaf parsley, extra torn leaves to garnish
sea salt and freshly ground black pepper

Bring a large pan of salted water to a rolling boil and then swirl in the spaghetti. Cook the pasta for 8–10 minutes, or until just tender but still with a little bite – al dente.

Meanwhile, heat the butter in a large pan over a low heat. Add the onion and garlic and cook for 5 minutes, until softened but not coloured, stirring frequently. Add the pancetta or bacon to the pan and cook for another 8–10 minutes, until crisp and golden, stirring continuously.

Pour the wine into the bacon mixture and reduce to about 1 tablespoon. Crack the eggs into a bowl and add the Parmesan cheese and cream. Season with plenty of freshly ground black pepper and beat until well combined.

Drain the pasta and return it to the pan, then tip in the onions and pancetta. Pour over the beaten egg mixture and add the parsley. Cook gently for 1 minute, until the sauce thickens slightly. Be careful not to overcook the sauce, or the eggs will scramble! Season to taste.

To serve, divide among warmed serving bowls and add a good grinding of black pepper to each one. Scatter over a little more Parmesan to serve.

DINNER PARTY

Coq au Vin

A classic French coq au vin is made with a cock bird, but I like to use chicken legs, which have an excellent flavour and are very good value for money. If you want to go all out on presentation, garnish the finished dish with heart-shaped croutons. Simply stamp or cut out heart shapes from slices of white bread and fry in a little oil until golden brown. Remove from the pan with tongs and immediately dip the end points into chopped parsley to coat. Serves 6

6 chicken legs
1–2 tbsp rapeseed oil
175g (6oz) piece of smoked bacon, rind removed and meat cut into strips
2 carrots, sliced
2 celery sticks, sliced
2 garlic cloves, finely chopped
1 onion, sliced
1 bottle red wine
2 tsp chopped fresh thyme
500ml (18fl oz) chicken stock (page 226)
25g (1oz) butter
18 baby pearl onions or small shallots, peeled
250g (9oz) button mushrooms, quartered
2 tbsp cornflour
2 tbsp roughly chopped fresh flat-leaf parsley
sea salt and freshly ground black pepper
creamy mashed potatoes (page 151) or crusty bread, to serve

Season the chicken legs all over. Heat 1 tablespoon of oil in a casserole dish with a lid over a medium heat. Add the bacon and sauté for 3–4 minutes, until lightly browned, stirring occasionally. Scoop out with a slotted spoon and place in a bowl. Set aside. Add 3 of the chicken legs, presentation side down, and cook for 3–4 minutes, until golden brown, turning occasionally. Transfer to a plate and repeat with the remaining chicken legs.

Increase the heat a little and add another tablespoon of oil if necessary. Add the carrots, celery, garlic and onion to the casserole dish and sauté for about 5 minutes, until golden brown, stirring occasionally. Pour in the red wine, add the thyme and bring to a simmer, then cook for 5 minutes, scraping the bottom of the pan with a wooden spoon to remove any sediment. Pour in the stock and return the chicken legs to the pan. Bring to a simmer, then cover and simmer for about 1 hour, or until the chicken is cooked through and completely tender.

Meanwhile, melt the butter in a frying pan. Add the baby pearl onions or shallots and sauté over a medium heat for 5 minutes, shaking the pan occasionally. Scoop out with a slotted spoon and add to the bowl with the reserved bacon. Tip the mushrooms into the pan and sauté for about 5 minutes, until tender. Add to the bacon and baby pearl onions and set aside.

When the chicken is cooked, carefully transfer the legs to a large plate and set aside. Strain the sauce into a large, clean pan, reserving the vegetables. Mix the cornflour with a little water, then whisk into the sauce. Return to the boil and then reduce to a simmer and cook for a few minutes, until thickened, whisking occasionally. Stir in the bacon, baby onions and mushrooms and simmer for 6–8 minutes, until heated through and the flavours have a chance to combine. Return the chicken and reserved vegetables to the casserole along with the parsley, nestling them into the sauce and cooking for another 5 minutes, until heated through. Season to taste.

To serve, transfer the coq au vin to a warmed serving dish and serve straight from the table onto warmed serving plates. Hand around the creamy mashed potatoes or crusty bread separately.

Duck Confit with Savoy Cabbage

You'll need about 1 litre (1 ¾ pints) of duck fat for this recipe, but if you don't have that much, you can easily use some peanut oil or chicken fat to top up the quantity. Of course, you could also use shop-bought duck or goose fat or reuse some that has been stored in the fridge.
Serves 6

6 duck legs
6–7 fresh thyme sprigs
6 star anise
1 garlic clove, sliced
4 tbsp sea salt flakes
1 orange, sliced and pips removed
1 litre (1 ¾ pints) duck fat (or peanut oil or chicken fat
  can be used as top-up; see note above)
honey and ginger sauce (page 229), to serve (optional)
champ (page 151), to serve (optional)

Cabbage:
1 tsp sesame seeds
knob of butter
1 tbsp olive oil
1 red onion, thinly sliced
1 garlic clove, crushed
175g (6oz) Savoy cabbage, core removed and thinly sliced
sea salt and freshly ground black pepper

To marinate the duck legs, place them in a single layer in a shallow non-metallic dish and scatter over the thyme, star anise, garlic and salt. Cover with clingfilm and place in the fridge overnight to allow the flavours to penetrate the duck.

Preheat the oven to 120°C (225°F/gas mark ¼).

Rinse the marinade off the duck legs and pat dry with kitchen paper. Return the duck legs to the dish and scatter the orange slices on top, then pour over the duck fat (if the fat doesn't completely cover the legs, top it up with peanut oil or chicken fat). Place in the oven and cook very gently for about 4 hours, until the legs are tender and the meat is almost falling off the bone. Remove from the heat and leave to cool in the fat. This can be made 2–3 days before serving and stored in the fridge.

When ready to serve, preheat the grill to low. Remove the duck confit and orange slices from the fat and brush off any excess. Arrange the duck legs on a grill rack, skin side up. Don't put the rack too close to the grill or the skin will burn. Cook for 10–15 minutes, until the skin is crisp and golden. Cook the orange slices for 3–4 minutes, turning halfway through – they should be just catching colour.

Meanwhile, cook the cabbage. Toast the sesame seeds in a dry frying pan until golden and tip onto a plate. Place the butter and oil in a pan over a high heat. Once the butter is foaming, add the onion and garlic and sauté on a fairly high heat for 2–3 minutes, until lightly coloured, tossing occasionally. Add the cabbage and cook for a further 3–4 minutes, adding 2–3 table-spoons of water if necessary, until just tender but still crunchy. Toss through the toasted sesame seeds, then season to taste and keep warm.

To serve, divide the Savoy cabbage among warmed wide-rimmed serving bowls and arrange the crispy duck confit on top. Place the caramelised orange slices to the side and have a sepa-rate warmed dish of the champ, if liked. Drizzle around the honey and ginger sauce to serve, if using.

Salmon with Citrus Butter En Croute

These are perfect for serving at a dinner party – just dust the bottom layer of pastry with a little semolina or polenta to prevent them from going soggy if you are making them more than 1 hour in advance. If you are buying pastry, look out for all-butter varieties, as the flavour is just so much better. **Serves 4**

50g (2oz) unsalted butter, softened
1 tbsp chopped fresh flat-leaf parsley
2 tsp chopped fresh tarragon
2 tsp chopped fresh dill
finely grated rind of ½ lemon
finely grated rind of ½ orange
500g (1lb 2oz) puff pastry, thawed if frozen
a little plain flour, for dusting

4 x 175g (6oz) organic salmon fillets (about 2.5cm (1in) thick), skinned and boned
50g (2oz) baby spinach leaves
1 egg yolk beaten with 1 tbsp milk
sea salt and freshly ground black pepper
peas with mint, to serve

Place the butter in a small bowl and beat in the parsley, tarragon, dill and lemon and orange rind and season generously. Spoon onto a sheet of clingfilm or non-stick parchment paper and shape into a roll about 2.5cm (1in) thick, then wrap tightly. Chill in the freezer for at least 10 minutes to firm up (or keep in the fridge for up to 48 hours until required, if time allows).

Preheat the oven to 200°C (400°F/gas mark 6). Line 2 baking sheets with parchment paper.

Cut the pastry into 8 even-sized sections and roll each one out on a lightly floured surface into a 12.5cm x 18cm (5in x 7in) rectangle, trimming down the edges if necessary. Arrange 4 of the rectangles on the lined baking sheets. Place a salmon fillet in the centre of each one and cover with the spinach leaves, then season to taste. Unwrap the citrus butter and cut into 16 x 0.5cm (¼in) thick slices. Arrange 4 slices in an overlapping layer on each piece of salmon.

Brush the edges of the pastry bases with a little of the egg wash and lay a second sheet of pastry on top, pressing down to seal. Crimp the edges by gently pressing the edge of the pastry with a fork. Continue all the way around the edge of the parcel. Repeat until you have 4 parcels in total. Season each one with a little salt and pepper.

Brush the pastry parcels with the remaining egg wash and bake for 25–30 minutes, until the pastry is cooked through and golden brown.

To serve, arrange the salmon parcels on warmed serving plates with some buttered peas with mint.

Moroccan Lamb Tagine

I like to make my tagines a little richer than is traditional in Morocco. This involves browning the meat, frying off the spices, reducing the sauce and cooking it all gently in the oven with the delicious Medjool dates. The flavour of this tagine only improves with time – just leave it to cool completely, then place in the fridge for up to 2 days. This also allows any excess fat to rise to the top so that it can be easily removed. Flaked almonds are sprinkled on top just before serving, as is the custom in the Middle East. Serves 6–8

2 tbsp hot paprika
1 tbsp ground coriander
1 tbsp turmeric
2 tsp ground cinnamon
2 tsp ground cumin
2 tsp coarse ground black pepper
1.5kg (3lb 5oz) lamb shoulder, well trimmed and cut into 4cm (1 ½in) chunks
4 garlic cloves, chopped
3 onions, roughly chopped
2.5cm (1in) piece of fresh root ginger, peeled and chopped
2 tbsp olive oil
450ml (¾ pint) tomato juice
450ml (¾ pint) chicken stock (page 226)
2 tbsp clear honey
225g (8oz) Medjool dates, cut in half and stones removed
50g (2oz) toasted flaked almonds
sea salt and freshly ground black pepper
fresh coriander leaves, to garnish
Greek yoghurt, to garnish

Couscous:
350g (12oz) couscous
6 tbsp extra virgin olive oil
juice of 2 lemons
600ml (1 pint) chicken stock (page 226)
sea salt and freshly ground black pepper
4 tbsp chopped fresh flat-leaf parsley
4 tbsp chopped fresh mint
½ pomegranate, seeds removed and all white pith discarded

Mix together the paprika, coriander, turmeric, cinnamon, cumin and pepper in a large bowl, then tip half into a small bowl and set aside. Add the lamb to the large bowl and coat in the spices. Cover with clingfilm and chill overnight, but up to 2 days is perfect.

Preheat the oven to 160°C (325°F/gas mark 3).

Place the garlic, onions and ginger into a food processor and pulse until finely minced. Heat a large heavy-based casserole over a medium heat. Add 1 tablespoon of oil and brown off the marinated lamb in batches. Add the remaining tablespoon of oil to the pan, then add the onion mixture and cook for a few minutes, until softened but not coloured. Stir in the reserved spice mixture and cook for another minute or so, until well combined.

Pour the tomato juice and stock into the pan and then add the browned lamb with the honey, stirring to combine. Bring to the boil, cover and transfer to the oven. Cook for 2 hours, stirring in the dates halfway through, until the lamb is completely tender and the sauce has thickened and reduced. Season to taste.

To make the couscous, place it in a large bowl. Add 4 tablespoons of oil and all the lemon juice. Mix well, ensuring that all the grains are completely coated. Heat the stock in a small pan and season generously. Pour the stock over the couscous and allow it to sit in a warm place for 6–8 minutes, until all the liquid has been absorbed.

To serve, stir the remaining 2 tablespoons of oil along with the herbs and pomegranate seeds into the couscous and fluff it up with a fork, then spoon into a warmed serving dish. Put the lamb tagine into a separate warmed dish and scatter over the toasted almonds and coriander leaves. Place the Greek yoghurt in a bowl with a spoon so that guests can help themsleves.

Moroccan Lamb Tagine

Braised Blade of Beef with Celeriac Purée

This is a perfect dinner party dish, as the braised beef blade can be made up to 2 days in advance, but it must be prepared at least 24 hours in advance to achieve a good shape. The sauce can also be prepared at the same time, as can the celeriac purée, leaving very little to do last minute except enjoy your guests! Serves 4

4 tbsp rapeseed oil
400g (14oz) piece of beef blade, well trimmed
2 carrots, cut into chunks
2 garlic cloves, crushed
1 onion, roughly chopped
900ml (1 ½ pints) beef stock (page 227)
300ml (½ pint) red wine
2 fresh thyme sprigs
2 fresh rosemary sprigs
1 tsp softened butter
sea salt and freshly ground black pepper

Celeriac purée:
275g (10oz) celeriac, peeled and cut into chunks
100ml (3 ½fl oz) cream
100ml (3 ½fl oz) vegetable stock (page 225)
20g (¾oz) butter

To garnish:
1 tbsp olive oil
1 smoked streaky bacon rasher, rind removed
1 slice of white bread, crusts removed and very finely diced
½ tsp snipped fresh chives

Preheat the oven to 180°C (350°F/gas mark 4).

To prepare the braised beef blade, heat 1 tablespoon of oil in a large casserole dish with a lid. Add the beef blade and brown all over for 3–4 minutes, turning regularly with tongs. Transfer to a plate. Add another tablespoon of oil to the casserole, reduce the heat a little and add the carrots, garlic and onion. Cook for a further 5 minutes, stirring, until golden brown.

Return the beef blade and any juices to the casserole and pour over the beef stock and red wine. Add the herbs and seasoning, then bring to the boil. Cover tightly with foil and a lid. Cook in the oven for 3 hours, until the beef is meltingly tender.

Carefully remove the beef from the braising juices and leave to rest on a warmed plate covered with foil. Strain the braising juices into a clean pan and bring to the boil, then reduce the heat and simmer for 25–30 minutes, until reduced by half to a sauce consistency. Leave to cool, then place in the fridge.

When the beef blade has cooled slightly, shred it into pieces on a double layer of clingfilm, discarding any fat. Roll up tightly to create a sausage shape about 5cm (2in) thick, tying the ends really tightly to make a good, firm shape. Place in the fridge overnight to firm up.

To prepare the garnishes, heat a large non-stick frying pan with the olive oil. When hot, add the bacon and cook until crisp and golden, turning once. Drain on kitchen paper and then dice very finely and place in a bowl. Next add the bread dice to the unwashed bacon pan and sauté until golden. Tip into the bowl with the bacon and add the chives, then mix well to combine. Set aside until needed.

To make the celeriac purée, place the celeriac in a pan with the cream and stock. Bring to the boil, then reduce the heat and simmer for 20–25 minutes, until the celeriac is soft. Once the celeriac is cooked, place the mixture into a blender and blitz until smooth. Add the butter and blitz again until smooth. Season to taste and keep warm if using immediately. Otherwise, cover and chill until needed.

To finish preparing the beef blade, trim off the ends and then cut into 4 even-sized pieces that are each about 2cm (¾in) thick and carefully remove the clingfilm. Heat a frying pan over a medium heat and add the remaining 2 tablespoons of oil along with the butter. Once the butter stops sizzling, add the pieces of beef blade to the pan and cook for 2 minutes on each side, until golden brown and crispy and completely warmed through.

Place a spoonful of the reserved bacon and crouton mixture on top of each piece of beef blade and keep warm. Place the reserved reduced braising juices in a pan and allow to warm through for the sauce.

To serve, spoon some celeriac purée into the centre of each warmed plate and add a piece of the garnished beef blade. Pour over some sauce and serve the rest separately in a gravy boat.

VEGETABLE SIDES

Creamy Mashed Potatoes

These mashed potatoes will keep warm in a very cool oven (120°C/250°F/gas mark ½) for up to 3 hours. Alternatively, leave to cool and then reheat gently using a little more butter. I think the red-skinned Rooster potatoes make the best mash, as they have a consistently floury texture and lovely smooth flavour. **Serves 4–6**

1.5kg (3lb) floury potatoes (such as
  Roosters), cut into even-sized chunks
about 120ml (4fl oz) milk and/or cream

100g (4oz) butter
1 tsp chopped fresh flat-leaf parsley
sea salt and freshly ground black pepper

Place the potatoes in a large pan of salted water. Bring to the boil, cover and simmer for 15–20 minutes, or until the potatoes are tender without breaking up. Drain and return to the pan over a low heat to dry out.

Mash the potatoes, or pass them through a potato ricer or vegetable mouli if you want a really smooth finish. Heat the milk and/or cream in a small pan. Using a wooden spoon, beat 75g (3oz) of the butter into the potatoes until it's melted and then beat in enough of the hot milk until you have achieved a smooth, creamy purée. Season to taste.

To serve, melt the remaining 25g (1oz) butter in a small pan or in the microwave. Put the creamy mashed potatoes into a warmed serving dish and spoon over the melted butter. Season with pepper and sprinkle over the parsley. Use as required.

Variations

Once mastered, this recipe can be adapted for different results. Try replacing a couple of tablespoons of the milk with crème fraîche or cream for a richer version. A couple of table-spoons of chives or a good dollop of Dijon mustard can also work well, depending on what you are serving with the mash.

Colcannon

Blanch half a head of shredded cabbage in a pan of boiling salted water for 2–3 minutes, then drain and quickly refresh. Add 2 finely chopped spring onions to the milk and/or cream while it's heating. Fold the cabbage into the mashed potato mixture and then gently reheat to serve.

Biarritz

Melt a good knob of butter in a frying pan and gently sauté a finely diced red pepper and small onion until softened, then beat into the mashed potato with 150g (5oz) finely chopped cooked ham and 2 tablespoons of chopped fresh flat-leaf parsley.

Champ

Heat 4 finely chopped spring onions with the milk and/or cream before beating into the mashed potatoes.

Crispy Roast Potatoes

For really crunchy roast potatoes with fluffy middles, choose a floury variety of potato, such as Roosters, and try to make sure that they are all similar in size. Save some fat that's left over from a roast to use for this dish. It really does make a world of difference, and as all fats freeze very well, there's no excuse not to have some, especially for special occasions like Christmas Day. To ensure really crispy roast potatoes, drain off any excess fat about 20 minutes before the end of the cooking time. This will help them to go really crispy and golden brown around the edges. Serves 4–6

1.5kg (3lb) floury potatoes (such as Roosters), halved
about 100ml (3 ½fl oz) sunflower oil, or dripping,
   goose or duck fat (see note above)
6 garlic cloves, slightly smashed (not peeled)
3 fresh rosemary sprigs
sea salt

Preheat the oven to 220°C (425°F/gas mark 7).

Place the potatoes in a pan of cold salted water and bring to the boil. Reduce the heat and simmer for 8–10 minutes, until the outsides have just softened. Drain and return to the pan for a minute to dry out, shaking vigorously to knock off all the hard edges.

Meanwhile, preheat a roasting tin with a 1cm (½in) depth of oil, dripping, duck or goose fat for a few minutes, until just smoking. Roughly prod the outside of the potatoes with a fork and toss them with the garlic and rosemary. Carefully tip them into the hot oil, basting the tops. Roast for about 45 minutes to 1 hour, turning occasionally, until crisp and golden.

To serve, transfer the crispy roast potatoes with a slotted spoon into a warmed serving bowl. Season with the salt and place them straight on the table or use as required.

French Beans with Hazelnuts and Garlic

These would also be delicious with two diced vine tomatoes that have been seeded. Simply add to the pan with the beans, but only in the summer, when tomatoes are at their best. **Serves 4–6**

350g (12oz) French green beans, trimmed
1 tbsp hazelnut oil or garlic rapeseed oil
1 small shallot, finely chopped
1 garlic clove, crushed
2 tsp chopped fresh flat-leaf parsley
25g (1oz) roasted skinned hazelnuts, chopped
sea salt and freshly ground black pepper

Plunge the French beans into a large pan of boiling salted water and return to the boil, then boil for a further 2 minutes, until just tender. Drain and refresh under cold running water.

Return the pan to the heat with the hazelnut or garlic rapeseed oil. Tip in the shallot and garlic and sauté for 2–3 minutes, until softened. Add the blanched beans and continue to sauté for 1–2 minutes, until just heated through. Sprinkle in the parsley and toss until well coated. Season to taste.

To serve, put the sautéed French beans into a warmed serving dish and scatter over the chopped hazelnuts or use as required.

Roasted Root Vegetables with Sesame Seeds

Roasting is a great way to cook root vegetables, as they're robust enough to cope with the intense heat, and the honey helps draw out the most wonderful flavours. Just make sure that all your vegetables are roughly the same size to ensure even cooking. Try using any combination of root vegetables you fancy. However, it's probably worth remembering that beetroot will stain all other root vegetables, so it's best to roast them on their own. Serves 4–6

2 tbsp rapeseed oil
450g (1lb) carrots, trimmed and halved lengthways
450g (1lb) large parsnips, trimmed, quartered and cored
1 tbsp clear honey
1 tsp toasted sesame seeds
1 tsp chopped fresh flat-leaf parsley
sea salt and freshly ground black pepper

Preheat the oven to 180°C (350°F/gas mark 4).

Place the oil in a large roasting tin and add the carrots and parsnips, tossing until well coated. Season generously. Roast for 30 minutes, then drizzle over the honey and toss to coat evenly. Roast for another 10 minutes, or until the vegetables are completely tender and lightly charred. Sprinkle over the sesame seeds and parsley and toss gently until evenly coated.

To serve, tip the roasted root vegetables into a warmed serving dish and place directly on the table or use as required.

Brussels Sprout Crumble

If you aren't a fan of Brussels sprouts, try using thickly sliced leeks with broccoli or cauliflower instead. This will also make a good vegetarian option as part of a Christmas lunch if you leave out the bacon. Serves 4–6

675g (1 ½lb) Brussels sprouts, trimmed and cut in half
25g (1 oz) butter, extra to grease
2 rindless smoked bacon rashers, diced
1 large red onion, thinly sliced
200ml (7fl oz) cream
50ml (2fl oz) milk
good pinch of freshly grated nutmeg
40g (1 ½oz) fresh white breadcrumbs
25g (1oz) walnut halves or pieces, chopped
15g (½oz) freshly grated Parmesan
1 tsp chopped fresh flat-leaf parsley
sea salt and freshly ground black pepper

Preheat the oven to 190°C (375°F/gas mark 5).

Half fill a pan with water, season with salt and bring to the boil. Add the Brussels sprouts and simmer for 4–5 minutes, until just tender but not soggy. Drain and refresh under running cold water.

Heat the butter in a pan and sauté the bacon and red onion over a medium heat for about 5 minutes, until the onion is softened and the bacon has begun to crisp up.

Butter a baking dish and tip in the blanched Brussels sprouts. Scatter over the sautéed bacon and red onion. Mix the cream with the milk and nutmeg in a jug and season to taste, then pour over the sprouts. Mix the breadcrumbs with the walnuts, Parmesan and parsley, then season to taste and sprinkle on top of the sprouts. Place in the oven for 20–25 minutes, until bubbling and golden brown.

To serve, place the Brussels sprout crumble straight on the table or use as required.

LUNCHBOX

Spiced Yoghurt Grilled Chicken Skewers

These spiced chicken skewers are completely delicious in a lunchbox served hot or cold. They would also be fantastic as part of a portable picnic spread or to cook on a disposable barbecue at the beach. **Serves 4**

250g Greek yoghurt
1 garlic clove, crushed
2 tbsp chopped fresh coriander
2 tbsp chopped fresh flat-leaf parsley
1 tsp paprika
1 tsp ground cumin
1 tsp finely grated lemon rind
good pinch of cayenne pepper
6 skinless, boneless chicken thighs, trimmed and quartered
rapeseed oil, for brushing
sea salt and freshly ground black pepper
flatbreads, to serve
lamb's lettuce, to serve
shop-bought hummus or roasted red pepper hummus (page 169), to serve
tomato and mint salad, to serve

Place the yoghurt, garlic, coriander, parsley, paprika, cumin, lemon rind and cayenne pepper in a bowl and mix to combine. Add the chicken pieces and stir until coated. Season with salt and pepper, then set aside for at least 10 minutes, or up to 24 hours covered with clingfilm in the fridge is perfect.

Heat a griddle pan. Thread 3 pieces of chicken onto a 10cm (4in) wooden bamboo skewer – you'll make 8 in total. Brush the griddle pan with the oil and cook the chicken skewers for 5–6 minutes on each side, until cooked through and lightly charred.

Wrap the chicken skewers in tin foil and put in lunchboxes with separately wrapped flatbreads. Put in small pots of lettuce, hummus and a tomato and mint salad, if liked.

To serve, arrange the flatbread on a plate with the chicken skewers and lettuce. Place the tomato and mint salad to the side with the pot of hummus.

Vietnamese Pot Noodles

This is what I love to eat when I'm feeling a bit under the weather but need my body to keep going. It's a fantastic way of filling you up for the day and literally takes no more than 10 minutes to prepare from start to finish. I like to bring it with me in a flask with a nice wide neck so that it's easy to eat. Check out the new generation of flasks available on the Internet, in good kitchen shops or even some supermarkets – they will keep your food nice and hot for at least 6 hours.
Serves 4

450g (1lb) straight-to-wok thin noodles
1.2 litres (2 pints) chicken stock (page 226)
1 tsp finely grated root ginger
200g (7oz) pak choi, cut on the diagonal into strips
150g (5oz) baby corn, halved and sliced on the diagonal
150g (5oz) mangetout, trimmed and sliced on the diagonal
1 tsp cornflour
4 tbsp dark soy sauce
1 tbsp sweet chilli sauce
juice of 1 lime
150g (5oz) fresh bean sprouts
fresh coriander, to garnish
fresh mint leaves, to garnish

Place the noodles in a heatproof bowl and pour over enough boiling water to cover. Set aside for 5 minutes, until softened, or as per the packet instructions.

Pour the stock into a large pan with the ginger and bring to the boil. Add the pak choi, baby corn and mangetout to the stock. Mix the cornflour with a little water in a bowl and then stir into the pan. Return to a simmer and cook for 2 minutes, until the vegetables are tender. Add the soy sauce, chilli sauce and lime juice, stirring to combine.

To serve, drain the noodles and divide among warmed flasks or bowls. Add the bean sprouts and ladle over the flavoured stock. Scatter coriander and mint leaves on top and eat with chopsticks and a spoon.

Variation

Cook 350g (12oz) minute steak or chicken fillets on a lightly oiled griddle pan, then cut into small pieces and arrange on top of the noodles.

Granola Bars

This is a great lunchbox option for children and adults alike. As dried fruit and nuts are an excellent source of energy, they should keep everyone happy until teatime. Eat them in the car if you're planning an early start or use for picnics as an excellent healthy option. Experiment by replacing the sultanas with dried cranberries, cherries or banana chips. Leave out peanut butter if you have any doubt about a nut allergy. **Makes 12 bars**

150g (5oz) porridge oats
75g (3oz) ready-to-eat apricots, chopped
50g (2oz) sultanas
50g (2oz) dried papaya or mango, finely chopped
50g (2oz) dates, pitted and roughly chopped
25g (1oz) flaked almonds
25g (1oz) sesame seeds
4 tbsp smooth peanut butter
3 tbsp clear honey
2 egg whites

Preheat the oven to 190°C (350°F/gas mark 5). Line a 27.5cm x 18cm (11in x 7in) baking tin with parchment paper.

Place the porridge oats in a bowl and stir in the apricots, sultanas, papaya or mango, dates, flaked almonds and sesame seeds.

Place the peanut butter and honey in a small pan and heat gently, stirring occasionally, until smooth. Drizzle into the oat mixture and mix well to combine.

Put the egg whites in a bowl and beat with a balloon whisk until light and frothy. Fold into the oat and honey mixture until everything is sticking together. Transfer to the prepared baking tin and spread out evenly, pressing down the mixture with the back of a spoon to make the surface as even as possible.

Bake for 20–25 minutes, until the top is golden brown and feels firm to the touch. Remove from the oven and cool slightly in the tin, then cut into 12 bars. Leave to cool completely before removing them from the tin.

To serve, store the bars in an airtight container for up to 5 days and wrap in greaseproof paper to pack for lunchboxes.

Prawn and Avocado Wrap

This is an updated version of the classic prawn mayonnaise sandwich, which is still one of the most popular shop-bought sandwiches. To change the filling, try using leftover roasted vegetables with feta or roast beef with a smear of onion marmalade and plenty of rocket. Experiment by trying the wide variety of different types of flatbreads available too. Serves 4

100g (4oz) mayonnaise
1 tbsp sweet chilli sauce
1 tbsp shredded fresh basil
½ lemon, pips removed
1 large, ripe Hass avocado
4 large deli wraps or soft flour tortillas
50g (2oz) wild rocket
200g (7oz) large cooked, peeled prawns
sea salt and freshly ground black pepper

Place the mayonnaise in a bowl and add the chilli sauce, basil and a good squeeze of the lemon juice. Season to taste and mix until well combined.

Cut the avocado in half and remove the stone, then cut into slices and place in a bowl. Drizzle in a squeeze of the lemon juice to prevent it from discolouring. Heat a heavy-based frying pan. Heat each deli wrap or soft flour tortilla for 30 seconds on the frying pan, turning once.

Spread the flavoured mayonnaise all over each of the heated wraps or tortillas and stack the rocket, avocado slices and prawns down the centre. Season to taste and roll up to enclose the filling.

To serve, cut each one on the diagonal and arrange on plates or wrap in greaseproof paper to pack for lunchboxes.

Variations

Egg Mayonnaise with Pistachio
Chop 4 hard-boiled eggs and combine in a bowl with 3 tablespoons of sour cream, 2 tablespoons of chopped pistachio nuts, 1 teaspoon of Dijon mustard, 12 ripped fresh basil leaves and season with salt and a pinch of paprika. Use to fill wraps or warmed pitta breads with plenty of fresh watercress.

Smoked Salmon and Cream Cheese

Mix a 200g (7oz) tub of cream cheese with 2 tablespoons of chopped fresh dill, 1 teaspoon of lemon juice and plenty of black pepper. Spread this mixture over 4 wraps and top with a layer of smoked salmon (you'll need about 350g (12oz) in total). Roll up like a Swiss roll to make a spiral look. Trim the ends, then wrap really tightly in clingfilm, twisting the ends tightly to enclose. Place in the fridge until you are ready to use. You can make these up to 1 day ahead. To serve, take a really sharp knife and cut on the diagonal to get a nice shape, then arrange on a plate with some wild rocket leaves.

Parma Ham, Rocket and Goat's Cheese

Mix 200g (7oz) of soft goat's cheese (curd) with plenty of black pepper. Spread this mixture over 4 wraps and scatter over 50g (2oz) of rocket, reserving a little to garnish. Top with a layer of thinly sliced Parma ham (about 175g (6oz) should be plenty) and roll up like a Swiss roll to make a spiral look. Trim the ends, then wrap really tightly in clingfilm, twisting the ends tightly to enclose. Place in the fridge until you are ready to use. You can make these up to 1 day ahead. To serve, take a really sharp knife and cut on the diagonal to get a nice shape, then arrange on a plate to serve.

Roasted Red Pepper Hummus Torpedos

This is a variation on traditional hummus and has a fantastic vibrant colour. Here it is served stuffed into pitta, but it would also be great spread on crackers or chunks of warm bread, or scooped up with tortilla chips. Serves 6

6 pitta breads
2 small carrots, grated
1 small cucumber, halved into half-moon shapes and sliced
good handful of salad leaves, such as baby spinach, rocket and/or watercress
about 1 tbsp extra virgin olive oil

Roasted red pepper hummus:
1 large red pepper
rapeseed oil
1 mild red chilli
400g (14oz) can chickpeas, drained and rinsed
2 garlic cloves, crushed
100ml (3 ½fl oz) tahini (sesame seed paste)
juice of 1 lemon
good pinch of ground cumin
sea salt and freshly ground black pepper

Preheat the oven to 200°C (400°F/gas mark 6).

To make the hummus, place the red pepper in a baking tin and drizzle with a little oil. Roast for 15 minutes, then add the chilli, drizzle over a little more oil and continue to cook for another 15–20 minutes, until the vegetables are completely tender and nicely charred. Transfer to a polythene bag and leave to cool completely (this will help to steam the skins off). When cool enough to handle, peel the red pepper and chilli and then cut in half and remove the cores. Roughly chop the remaining flesh.

Place the red pepper and chilli flesh in a food processor. Add the chickpeas, garlic, tahini, lemon juice, cumin and 4 tablespoons of water. Whizz to a creamy purée. Add more garlic, lemon juice, cumin or salt and pepper to taste. Turn out into a bowl.

To serve, warm the pitta breads under the grill, turning once, then split open and fill the bottom with the carrot, cucumber and salad leaves. Fill with the roasted red pepper hummus and drizzle with a little extra virgin olive oil. Season with pepper and wrap in tin foil, then place each pitta in a lunchbox and use as required.

Variations

Spinach and Feta Hummus Pitta
Omit the red pepper and chilli from the hummus and add some sautéed spinach and feta to the food processor instead.

Hummus and Turkey Pitta
Just make regular hummus and add some thinly sliced cooked turkey to the pitta breads.

Roasted Mediterranean Vegetable and Hummus Pitta
Add some roasted Mediterranean vegetables to the pitta breads instead of the carrot and cucumber.

KIDS' FAVOURITES

Ham, Cheese and Tomato French Toast

Sometimes children arrive in starving and you need something that can literally be ready in minutes. This certainly fits the bill and the fillings can be changed to suit their moods. Experiment with crispy bacon or prosciutto instead of the ham, and if your children have a sophisticated palate, try using a mixture of ricotta and Parmesan spiked with shredded basil. **Serves 4**

4 slices hand-carved cooked ham
8 thick slices white bread
125g (4 ½oz) Cheddar cheese, grated
2 ripe tomatoes, sliced
4 eggs, lightly beaten
25g (1oz) freshly grated Parmesan
4 tbsp milk
butter, for cooking
sea salt and freshly ground black pepper
lightly dressed green salad, to serve
tomato relish, to serve

Preheat the oven to 180°C (350°F/gas mark 4).

Arrange the ham on half of the slices of bread and divide the Cheddar on top. Arrange the tomato slices on the Cheddar and season to taste, then cover with the remaining slices of bread.

Place the eggs, Parmesan and milk in a shallow dish and whisk to combine. Dip the sandwiches, one at a time, in the egg mixture for 30 seconds on each side.

Melt a little butter in a large non-stick frying pan. Add the sandwiches in batches (this will depend on the size of your pan) and cook for 1–2 minutes on each side, or until lightly golden. Transfer to a grill rack set on a roasting tray and cook in the oven for another 4–6 minutes, or until the cheese is melted in the centre and the French toast is golden brown.

To serve, cut each ham, cheese and tomato French toast in half and arrange on serving plates with the salad and a dollop of tomato relish.

Crispy Fish Tacos with Tomato Salsa

This is a great recipe to get children to eat fish in a novel way. You can use any firm-fleshed white fish, such as coley, whiting or haddock, or even raw, peeled Dublin Bay prawns would be delicious. Serves 4

2 x 350g (12oz) hake fillets, skinned
  and boned
vegetable oil, for deep-frying
8 soft flour tortillas
2 Little Gem lettuces, finely shredded
300ml (½ pint) sour cream
sea salt and freshly ground black pepper
lime wedges, to garnish

Batter:
50g (2oz) plain flour
25g (1oz) cornflour
175ml (6fl oz) sparking water, well chilled

Tomato salsa:
4 ripe tomatoes, skinned, seeded and
  finely chopped
1 small red onion, finely chopped
juice of 1 lime
2 tbsp chopped fresh coriander
pinch of caster sugar

To make the tomato salsa, place the tomatoes in a bowl with the red onion, lime juice, coriander and sugar. Season to taste, then stir well to combine and set aside at room temperature to allow the flavours to develop.

To make the batter, place the flour, cornflour, sparkling water and a pinch of salt into a food processor and blend until smooth. Cut the hake fillets into 1cm (½in) strips and season generously.

Pour the vegetable oil into a pan until it's about one-third full and heat to 190°C (375°F), or until a small piece of white bread dropped into the oil browns and rises to the surface in 1 minute. Warm the tortillas in a low oven or in the microwave as per the packet instructions.

Dip the strips of the fish into the batter, shaking off any excess, and then drop them into the hot oil. Cook for 3–4 minutes, until crisp and golden brown. Lift out with a slotted spoon and drain briefly on kitchen paper.

To serve, put some lettuce down the centre of each warmed flour tortilla and spoon over the tomato salsa, then top with the crispy hake goujons and the sour cream. Add a squeeze of lime and then fold in the sides of the tortilla. Roll it up as tightly as you can to eat.

Crispy Chicken Schnitzel Baps

This recipe makes a little chicken go a long way and is the ultimate chicken burger for children. It doesn't take long to prepare, especially if you have some breadcrumbs tucked away in the freezer. Serves 4

25g (1oz) seasoned flour
1 large egg
1 tbsp milk
pinch of salt
50g (2oz) fresh white breadcrumbs
2 tbsp freshly grated Parmesan
2 large skinless chicken fillets
2 tbsp olive oil
knob of butter
4 white bread rolls
sea salt and freshly ground black pepper

Coleslaw:
2 carrots, finely grated
¼ head of white cabbage, tough core removed and shredded
4 tbsp mayonnaise

Put the seasoned flour on a flat plate. Beat the egg, milk and a pinch of salt in a shallow dish. Put the breadcrumbs and Parmesan in a separate shallow dish, then season with salt and pepper.

Cut each chicken fillet in half so that it almost opens out like a butterfly, then cut all the way through – you're looking to get 2 even-sized, thin pieces of chicken from each breast. Dust in the seasoned flour, shaking off any excess, then dip in the beaten egg and then coat in the breadcrumbs.

Heat a large non-stick frying pan over a medium heat. Add the oil and then add the butter. Once the butter stops sizzling, add in the coated chicken pieces and sauté for 2–3 minutes on each side, until cooked through and golden brown.

Meanwhile, to make the coleslaw, put the carrots and cabbage in a bowl and fold in the mayonnaise, then season to taste. Split the bread rolls in half and lightly toast them.

To serve, spread the bottom halves of the bread rolls with the coleslaw and put a crispy chicken schnitzel on top. Cover with the toasted bread roll tops.

Fresh Fruit Skewers with Marshmallows and Chocolate Fondue

This is a great way to serve a large number of children a yummy dessert that's not all bad! Use a selection of fruit that's in season and watch them disappear... **Serves 4–6**

8 large chunks of fresh pineapple
4 strawberries, hulled and halved
4 large white marshmallows
4 large pink marshmallows
2 apples, cored and quartered
2 large bananas, peeled and quartered
2 plums, stoned and quartered
2 kiwi fruit, peeled and quartered

Chocolate fondue:
100g milk chocolate, broken into pieces
2 tbsp cream
knob of butter
1–2 tbsp boiling water

To make the chocolate fondue, place the chocolate, cream and butter in a small pan or put in a bowl in the microwave. Cook over a gentle heat until melted, stirring occasionally. Add the boiling water to loosen the fondue if you think it's necessary.

Meanwhile, thread the different fruits and marshmallows onto 8 wooden skewers.

To serve, pour the chocolate fondue into small serving bowls and set on plates, then balance the fruit and marshmallow skewers on each one.

Monster Cookie Ice Cream Sandwiches

These are perfect for handing out to children at the end of a barbecue or family gathering. If you don't want to serve them immediately, they can be wrapped tightly in clingfilm and frozen until needed. It's also a nice idea to roll the sides of the ice cream cookie sandwiches in hundreds and thousands or a crumbled-up chocolate. **Makes 10**

375g (13oz) light muscovado sugar
225g (8oz) butter, at room temperature
2 eggs
2 tsp vanilla extract
350g (12oz) plain flour
1 tsp baking powder
1 tsp bread soda
½ tsp salt
150g (5oz) Smarties
2 x 500ml (18fl oz) cartons vanilla ice cream

Preheat the oven to 180°C (350°F/gas mark 4). Line 4 baking sheets with parchment paper.

Using a hand-held mixer, cream the sugar and butter in a large bowl until soft and fluffy. Whisk the eggs lightly with the vanilla extract and then gradually beat into the butter mixture. Sieve the flour, baking powder, bread soda and salt into a separate bowl, then beat into the butter and egg mixture.

Use dampened hands to shape the cookie mixture into 20 even-sized balls and then arrange on the lined baking sheets. Flatten the balls slightly, allowing plenty of room for spreading (aim for 4 balls of dough per sheet; you'll need to bake the cookies in batches). Dot with the Smarties and bake for 10–12 minutes, until rich golden all over and firm at the edges but still a little soft to the touch in the centre. Leave to cool a little, then using a metal fish slice or spatula, carefully transfer to a wire rack while they are still hot (otherwise they tend to stick). Leave to cool.

To serve, place a scoop of ice cream on the flat side of half of the cookies. Cover with the rest of the cookies and then press each one down gently to make a sandwich.

DESSERTS

Fruity Bread and Butter Pudding

An Irish country kitchen classic that should have a soft set texture with an exquisitely light spicing of nutmeg and vanilla, a few finely chopped prunes and sultanas and a wonderful buttery top. To make it even more delicious, try making it with day-old croissants or brioche. Serves 4–6

4 eggs
300ml (½ pint) milk
150ml (¼ pint) cream
finely grated rind and juice of 1 lemon
1 vanilla pod, split and seeds scraped out
50g (2oz) caster sugar
250g (9oz) sliced white bread (6 slices)
75g (3oz) butter, softened, extra for greasing
75g (3oz) ready-to-eat dried prunes, finely chopped
75g (3oz) sultanas
good pinch of freshly grated nutmeg
4 tbsp marmalade
icing sugar, to dust
pouring cream or vanilla ice cream, to serve

Preheat the oven to 180°C (350°F/gas mark 4). Lightly butter an ovenproof dish that's about 25cm x 16cm (10in x 6in) and 2.5cm (1in) deep.

Beat the eggs, milk and cream together in a large jug. Mix together the lemon rind and juice, vanilla seeds and sugar in a small bowl and then add to the egg mixture, beating lightly to combine.

Spread the slices of bread with the softened butter and cut off the crusts, then cut into triangles. Scatter half of the prunes and sultanas into the bottom of the buttered dish and arrange a layer of the bread triangles on top. Pour over half of the egg mixture, pressing the bread down gently, then repeat the layers with the remaining ingredients and sprinkle the nutmeg on top.

Place the dish into a roasting tin and fill with warm water until it comes three-quarters of the way up the dish. Bake for 30–35 minutes, until just set.

Meanwhile, sieve the marmalade and then heat it in a small pan. Brush the top of the cooked pudding with the marmalade to form a nice glaze when it comes out of the oven. Dust lightly with icing sugar.

To serve, cut into slices while still warm and arrange on warmed serving plates with pouring cream or ice cream.

Raspberry and White Chocolate Pavlova with Lemon and Mint

This is a variation of a recipe handed down to me by my mother, Vera. Mum was a great cook, and at one stage ran the restaurant as well as cooking for a family of nine. She loved to cook this dessert at family get-togethers. You can enjoy this all year around, using whatever fruits are in season. Feel free to make it the day before, but don't fill it until you are nearly ready to serve. A good pavlova should have a gooey, sticky centre, almost like a marshmallow. Serves 6–8

Pavlova:
4 large egg whites, at room temperature
pinch of salt
225g (8oz) caster sugar
2 tsp cornflour
1 tsp white wine vinegar
½ tsp vanilla extract

Filling:
400ml (14fl oz) cream
50g (2oz) icing sugar, sifted
1 vanilla pod, split in half and seeds
  scraped out
finely grated rind of 1 lemon
250g (9oz) raspberries
fresh mint sprigs, to decorate
white chocolate curls (page 231),
  to decorate

Preheat the oven to 150°C (300°F/gas mark 2). Line a baking sheet with parchment paper and draw on a 23cm (9in) circle. Flip the paper over so that the pencil doesn't transfer to the bottom of the pavlova.

Make the meringue in a large, clean, dry bowl. Whisk the egg whites and salt into stiff peaks. Slowly add the sugar, a third at a time, whisking well between each addition, until the mixture is stiffened and shiny. Sprinkle in the cornflour, vinegar and vanilla extract, then fold in gently with a metal spoon.

Pile the meringue onto the paper circle and make a deep hollow in the centre. Put in the oven and reduce the heat to 120°C (250°F/gas mark ½). Bake for 1 ½ hours, until pale brown but a little soft in the centre. Turn off the oven, leave the door ajar and allow to cool completely.

To make the filling, whip the cream in a bowl with the icing sugar, vanilla seeds and lemon rind until thickened and just holding its shape.

To serve, peel the parchment paper off the pavlova and carefully transfer to a serving plate or cake stand. Pile on the whipped cream and arrange the raspberries on top, then decorate with the mint sprigs and white chocolate curls. Serve straight to the table in all its glory.

Apple Tart with Custard

Homemade apple tart – a winning combination of delicate sweet pastry filled with heavenly scented apples – simply can't be beaten. To ring in the changes, mix the apples with blackberries or try a mixture of rhubarb and strawberry. To make your tart extra special, add a vanilla pod to your bag of sugar and leave for at least a week before using. **Serves 6–8**

Pastry:
225g (8oz) plain flour, extra for dusting
2 tbsp icing sugar
100g (4oz) butter, diced and chilled
2 large egg yolks
2–3 tablespoons ice-cold water

Filling:
900g (2lb) Bramley cooking apples
100g (4oz) caster sugar
¼ tsp ground cinnamon
good pinch of ground cloves
1 tbsp milk

Custard:
5 egg yolks
3 tbsp caster sugar
½ vanilla pod, split in half and seeds scraped out
300ml (½ pint) milk
100ml (3 ½fl oz) cream

To make the pastry, sift the flour and icing sugar into a bowl. Using a round-bladed knife or the tips of your fingers, work in the butter and then mix in the egg yolks with enough of the ice-cold water, until the dough just comes together. Wrap in clingfilm and chill for at least 30 minutes.

Preheat the oven to 190°C (375°F/gas mark 5). Lightly dust the work surface with flour.

Divide the pastry into 2 portions, one slightly larger than the other, then roll out the larger piece until it's about 30cm (12in) in diameter. Use to line a 20cm (8in) pie dish or a 23cm (9in) flat plate, gently pressing into the corners. Trim the edges with a knife and reserve the excess for decorating. Place back in the fridge to chill while you prepare the apples.

Peel, core and slice the apples. Place in a large bowl with all but 1 tablespoon of the caster sugar. Add the cinnamon and cloves and mix together. Brush the edge of the pastry with a little milk and then pile the apples into the lined pie dish. Roll out the second piece of pastry into a circle slightly larger than the pie dish and use to cover the apples. Press the edges together to seal, then use a sharp knife to cut away any excess.

Crimp the edges of the tart with a round-bladed knife and using your fingers as a guide. Roll out the pastry scraps and cut into leaf shapes. Brush the shapes with milk and stick on top of the pie. Brush the entire top of the pastry with milk and sprinkle over the remaining 1 tablespoon of sugar. Bake for 25–30 minutes, then reduce the oven to 180°C (350°F/gas mark 4) and bake for another 20–25 minutes, until golden brown.

Meanwhile, to make the custard, place the egg yolks in a large bowl with the sugar and vanilla seeds. Whisk with an electric mixer for a few minutes, until pale and thickened.

Place the milk and cream in a medium pan and bring to the boil, then immediately remove from the heat. Gradually whisk the heated milk and cream into the egg yolk mixture until smooth, then pour back into the pan and place over a gentle heat. Cook gently for 6–8 minutes on a medium heat, stirring constantly, until the custard coats the back of a wooden spoon. Keep warm.

To serve, cut the warm apple tart into slices and arrange on warmed serving plates with some of the custard. Put the remainder into a jug on the table.

Apple Tart with Custard

Lemon Meringue Pie

Lemon Meringue Pie

As this pastry is so short, it's in danger of breaking up when you are trying to roll it out. If this happens, try coarsely grating it directly into the tin and then quickly pressing the pastry up the sides and into the shape of the tin. No one will ever know the difference! Serves 6–8

Pastry:
175g (6oz) plain flour, extra for dusting
100g (4oz) butter, chilled and diced, extra for greasing
50g (2oz) caster sugar
pinch of salt
1 egg yolk
½ tbsp cream

Filling:
finely grated rind and juice of 3 lemons
4 tbsp cornflour
175g (6oz) caster sugar
50g (2oz) butter, softened
4 egg yolks

Meringue:
3 egg whites
150g (5oz) caster sugar

whipped cream, to serve

To make the pastry, place the flour, butter, sugar and salt into a food processor and blend for 20 seconds. Add the egg yolk and cream and blend again until the dough just comes together. Do not overwork or the pastry will be tough. Wrap in clingfilm and chill for 1 hour.

Thinly roll out the pastry into a buttered 20cm (8in) fluted loose-bottomed flan tin that's about 3cm (1 ¼in) deep. Trim the edges and prick the base with a fork, then chill for 30 minutes.

Preheat the oven to 200°C (400°F/gas mark 6).

Line the pastry case with tin foil or non-stick parchment paper and a thin layer of baking beans. Bake for 15–20 minutes, until golden. Reduce the oven temperature to 180°C (350°F/gas mark 4). Remove the pastry case from the oven and carefully remove the foil and beans, then return to the oven for 3–5 minutes, until lightly golden.

Meanwhile, to make the filling, place the lemon rind and 400ml (14fl oz) of water in a pan and bring to the boil. Remove from the heat and leave to stand for 30 minutes. Strain out and discard the lemon rind and then stir in the lemon juice. Blend the cornflour with a little of the lemon liquid to form a smooth paste, then add to the pan with the sugar and stir well. Bring to the boil, stirring continuously. Reduce the heat and cook for 2–3 minutes, stirring until thickened. Remove from the heat and stir in the butter until combined. Leave to cool a little and then beat in the egg yolks. Return to a low heat and cook for another 6–8 minutes, stirring constantly, until the mixture coats the back of a spoon. Pour into the pastry case and leave to cool completely.

Once cool, make the meringue. Place the egg whites in a large bowl and whisk into soft peaks, then gradually whisk in the sugar a spoonful at a time to make a stiff, glossy meringue. Spoon on top of the filling, spreading it out to make sure it makes a good seal with the pastry edge. Swirl the top of the meringue with the tip of a knife and bake for 15 minutes, until lightly golden and crisp on top. Leave to cool slightly and then carefully remove the tart from the tin and leave to cool for up to 2 hours – any longer and the meringue will start to weep.

To serve, cut the lemon meringue pie into slices and arrange on serving plates with dollops of whipped cream.

Mango and Lime Cheesecake

This cheesecake combines a luscious tropical fruit topping with a creamy filling and a spiced biscuit base. I think gelatine leaves are much easier to use than powdered gelatine. They are available now from most supermarkets, but if you can't find them, use 2 teaspoons of powdered gelatine for the filling and dissolve in 2 tablespoons of very hot water and use 1 teaspoon for the topping and dissolve in 1 tablespoon of very hot water. **Serves** 8

Base:
200g (7oz) ginger nut biscuits
100g (4oz) butter, melted
vegetable oil, for greasing

Filling:
4 gelatine leaves
175ml (6fl oz) milk
1 vanilla pod, split in half and seeds scraped out
175g (6oz) caster sugar
500g (18 oz) Greek yoghurt
finely grated rind and juice of 2 limes
150ml (¼ pint) cream

Topping:
2 gelatine leaves
400g (14oz) can mango slices in syrup, drained

fresh mint sprigs, to decorate
lightly whipped cream, to serve

To make the base, place the biscuits in a food processor or liquidiser and blend to fine crumbs. With the motor still running, pour in the melted butter through the feeder tube and mix until well combined. Tip into a lightly oiled 23cm (9in) loose-bottomed cake tin and press firmly and evenly to form a base for the cheesecake. Chill for at least 10 minutes, until firmly set, or up to 24 hours is fine.

Meanwhile, to make the filling, soak the gelatine leaves in a bowl of cold water for 10 minutes. Place the milk in a pan and add the vanilla seeds, whisking to combine. Cook until it just reaches boiling point, but do not allow to boil. Gently squeeze the gelatine dry and add to the pan with the sugar, whisking until the gelatine and sugar are both dissolved. Pour into a large bowl and leave to cool a little.

Stir the Greek yoghurt into the cooled milk mixture with the lime rind and juice. Whip the cream in a separate bowl until it's just holding its shape, then fold into the filling mixture. Pour into the set biscuit base and chill for at least 1 hour, until set, or up to 24 hours is fine.

To make the topping, soak the gelatine leaves in a bowl of cold water for 10 minutes. Place the mango slices in a mini processor or liquidiser and blend until smooth. Heat 1 tablespoon of water in a small pan or in the microwave. Gently squeeze the gelatine dry and stir into the hot water, until dissolved. Add to the mango purée and pour over the set cheesecake filling, spreading evenly with the back of a spoon. Chill for another 2–3 hours, until completely set, or up to 24 hours is fine.

To serve, remove the cheesecake from the tin and transfer to a serving plate, then decorate with the mint sprigs. Cut into slices and arrange on serving plates with a dollop of whipped cream.

BAKING

Mairead's Strawberry and Lemon Curd Sponge Cake

This recipe was given to me by my good friend Mairead Lavery, who looks after my column at the *Irish Farmers Journal*. It's what she whips up when visitors are coming in the door and she has nothing nice in the cupboard. It can be on the table in 20 minutes. It's delicious with any fresh fruit, such as raspberries, strawberries or even a drained can of peach slices; whatever you have to hand, really! **Serves 6**

knob of butter, for greasing
5 eggs, at room temperature
150g (5oz) caster sugar
1 vanilla pod, split in half and seeds removed
175g (6oz) self-raising flour, sifted
250g (9oz) strawberries
150ml (¼ pint) cream
5 tbsp good-quality lemon curd
icing sugar, to dust

Preheat the oven to 180°C (350°F/gas mark 4). Lightly grease 2 x 20cm (8in) sponge cake tins with butter.

Place the eggs, sugar and vanilla seeds in a good-sized bowl. Using either a hand-held or electric whisk, beat the mixture until it fills over half the bowl and has the consistency of lightly whipped cream.

Using a dessertspoon, gently fold in the sifted flour and continue folding until all the flour is fully absorbed. Divide the mixture between the prepared tins. Cook for 10–12 minutes. The cake is cooked when it comes slightly away from the tin. Turn out onto wire racks and leave to cool completely.

To serve, hull the strawberries, dice two-thirds and cut the remainder into quarters. Whip the cream in a bowl until soft peaks form. Spread the lemon curd on top of one of the cakes almost but not quite to the edge and scatter over the diced strawberries, then cover with half of the whipped cream. Carefully place the other sponge on top to cover the filling completely. Add a light dusting of icing sugar and place on a cake stand. Put the rest of the cream into a piping bag and pipe rosettes around the edge of the cake, then top each one with a strawberry quarter. Put straight on the table.

Sultana and Lemon Scones

These scones can be frozen on a baking sheet once they have been cut out. Once frozen, transfer them to a ziplock bag and freeze for up to 1 month. To cook from frozen, simply brush with egg wash and bake for 20–25 minutes. Makes 14–16

450g (1lb) self-raising flour, extra for dusting
generous pinch of salt
pinch of baking powder
50g (2oz) caster sugar
100g (4oz) unsalted butter, diced, extra to grease
2 eggs
50ml (2fl oz) cream
200ml (7fl oz) milk, extra if needed
4 handfuls sultanas
finely grated rind of 1 lemon
whipped cream, to serve (optional)
raspberry jam, to serve (optional)

Preheat the oven to 180°C (350°F/gas mark 4).

Sift the flour into a bowl with the salt and baking powder and then stir in the sugar. Using your fingertips, rub in the butter until the mixture resembles fine breadcrumbs.

Make a well in the centre and add 1 lightly beaten egg, the cream and enough milk to moisten, then add the sultanas and lemon rind. Mix well, until it has a soft doughy texture, but it should not be too moist. Add a little more milk if you think it's necessary.

Gather the dough into a ball and turn it out onto a floured surface, then roll lightly with a rolling pin to a 2.5cm (1in) thickness. Cut out rounds using a 6cm (2 ½in) fluted cutter and transfer onto a greased baking sheet.

Lightly beat the remaining egg with 1 tablespoon of water to make the glaze and brush it over the tops. Bake for 15 minutes, until the scones are well risen and golden brown. Transfer to a wire rack and leave to cool for at least 10 minutes.

To serve, put the scones on serving plates with small pots of whipped cream and raspberry jam, if you like.

Raspberry Chocolate Brownie with Salted Caramel Sauce

There is definitely something about chocolate that's addictive. It contains several stimulants, including caffeine and pleasure-inducing endorphins. These are intensely chocolatey brownies, which get smothered in a salted caramel sauce. If the brownies have gone cold and you want to heat them up in a hurry, pour over some of the sauce and flash under a hot grill until bubbling. **Makes 16**

Brownies:
400g (14oz) plain chocolate, finely
  chopped (at least 55% cocoa solids)
225g (8oz) butter, diced
4 eggs
275g (10oz) caster sugar
100g (4oz) self-raising flour
75g (3oz) cocoa powder
100g (4oz) toasted pecan nuts, roughly
  chopped

200g (7oz) raspberries
vanilla ice cream, to serve

Salted caramel sauce:
100g (4oz) caster sugar
75g (3oz) butter
250ml (9fl oz) cream
½ vanilla pod, split in half and
  seeds scraped out
1 tsp sea salt flakes

Preheat the oven to 160°C (325°F/gas mark 3). Line a 30cm x 20cm (12in x 8in) deep-sided baking tin with parchment paper.

Place 100g (4oz) of the chocolate in a heatproof bowl with the butter. Set the bowl over a pan of simmering water until the chocolate and butter have melted, then stir to combine. Remove from the heat and leave to cool a little.

Meanwhile, whisk the eggs in a bowl until they're stiff and holding their shape, then whisk in the sugar until you have achieved a stiff sabayon that can hold a trail of the figure eight. Sift the flour and cocoa powder into the sabayon and lightly fold them in. Add the melted chocolate mixture with the remaining finely chopped chocolate and the pecan nuts, and continue folding gently until all the ingredients are just combined. Finally, gently fold in the raspberries.

Pour the batter into the lined baking tin. Bake for 35–40 minutes, until the top is crusty but the centre is still a little soft.

Meanwhile, make the salted caramel sauce. Place the sugar in a pan with 150ml (¼ pint) of water. Bring to the boil, then reduce to a simmer and cook for about 15 minutes, until golden brown, without stirring. Stir in the butter, cream, vanilla seeds and salt and mix well over a low heat until it's a thick sauce consistency. Serve hot or leave to cool until needed.

To serve, remove the brownies from the oven and allow to cool in the tin for about 5 minutes, then remove from the tin and peel off the parchment paper. Reheat the salted caramel sauce in the pan. Cut the brownies into 16 rectangles and arrange on serving plates with the hot salted caramel sauce and scoops of ice cream.

Peanut Butter Cookies

These biscuits are completely delicious with a cup of tea or coffee and children seem to absolutely love them too. Makes 24

100g (4oz) light muscovado sugar
75g (3oz) butter, softened
100g (4oz) crunchy peanut butter
1 large egg, beaten
175g (6oz) plain flour, extra for dusting
¾ tsp bread soda
75g (3oz) unsalted peanuts
50g (2oz) Demerara sugar

Preheat the oven to 180°C (350°F/gas mark 4).

Place the muscovado sugar and butter in a bowl and whisk with a hand-held beater until light and fluffy. Mix in the peanut butter and then the egg until just combined. Fold in the flour and bread soda and then mix in the unsalted peanuts.

Put the Demerara sugar on a plate. Lightly flour your hands and roll the cookie dough into walnut-sized balls, then dip in the sugar, pressing the ball down gently. Flip it over and place on non-stick baking sheets, leaving room for expansion. Bake in batches for 12–15 minutes, or until the cookies are firm and lightly golden.

Leave the cookies to cool for a couple of minutes on the baking sheet and then transfer to a wire rack with a palette knife and leave to cool completely.

To serve, arrange the peanut butter cookies on a large serving platter.

Variation

White Chocolate and Pecan Nut
Use smooth peanut butter and fold in 175g (6oz) white chocolate drops and use roughly chopped pecan nuts instead of the unsalted peanuts.

Irish Tea Bread

This keeps very well wrapped in clingfilm and then in tin foil. The leftovers can be made into bread and butter puddings with a dash of Coole Swan Irish Cream liqueur or even just a simple French toast works well.

Makes 1 loaf

100g (4oz) sultanas
100g (4oz) currants or raisins
50g (2oz) glace cherries, chopped
50g (2oz) cut mixed peel
good splash of Irish whiskey
300ml (½ pint) strong hot tea
225g (8oz) light muscovado sugar
a little sunflower oil, for greasing
275g (10oz) self-raising flour
good pinch of freshly ground nutmeg
1 egg, beaten
1 tbsp clear honey
butter, to serve

Place the sultanas in a large bowl with the currants or raisins, glace cherries, mixed peel and whiskey. Pour over the tea and then stir in the sugar until it's dissolved. Cover with a plate and leave overnight to allow all the fruit to plump up.

Preheat the oven to 150°C (300°F/gas mark 2). Lightly grease a 900g (2lb) non-stick loaf tin with sunflower oil, then base line with parchment paper.

Sieve the flour and nutmeg into a bowl, then stir it into the soaked fruit mixture with the egg until evenly combined. Turn into the prepared tin and level the surface. Bake for 1 ½ hours, or until well risen and firm to the touch. A fine skewer inserted into the centre should come out clean.

Allow the tea bread to cool in the tin for about 10 minutes before turning it out. Brush the top with the honey, then leave to cool completely on a wire rack.

To serve, cut the tea brack into slices and spread with butter. Arrange on a serving platter.

BREAD

MacNean Wheaten Bread

At MacNean Restaurant we have experimented with a lot of recipes over the years and this is definitely the best I've tasted to date. It has a lovely sweet flavour but is still very much a savoury bread. It's the first thing my breakfast chef makes in the morning so that the smell wafts around the hotel, giving our guests a sense of things to come. **Makes 2 loaves**

450g (1lb) wholemeal flour
100g (4oz) strong white bread flour, extra for dusting
2 tsp bread soda
2 tsp salt
25g (1oz) light muscovado sugar
600ml (1 pint) buttermilk, extra if needed
3 tbsp sunflower seeds
2 tbsp golden syrup
4 tsp melted butter, extra for greasing and serving
handful of porridge oats, to decorate
1 tbsp pumpkin seeds, to decorate
1 tbsp sesame seeds, to decorate

Preheat the oven to 200°C (400°F/gas mark 6). Grease 2 x 600ml (1 pint) loaf tins.

Sift the flours, bread soda and salt into a bowl. Make a well in the centre and add the sugar, buttermilk, sunflower seeds, golden syrup and melted butter. Using a large spoon, mix gently and quickly until you have achieved a nice dropping consistency. Add a little bit more buttermilk if necessary, until the mixture binds together without being sloppy.

Divide the mixture equally between the prepared loaf tins and sprinkle over the porridge oats and pumpkin and sesame seeds. Bake for 40 minutes, until cooked through and each loaf has a slightly cracked crusty top, checking halfway through the cooking time that the loaves aren't browning too much. If they are, reduce the temperature or move the loaves down in the oven.

To check that the loaves are properly cooked, tip each one out of the tin and tap the base – it should sound hollow. If it doesn't, return it to the oven for another 5 minutes. Tip out onto a wire rack and leave to cool completely.

To serve, place the wheaten bread on a breadboard and cut into slices at the table. Hand around with a separate pot of butter for spreading.

Cheese and Onion Bread

This is a recipe for a classic white loaf, but here I've added a spoonful of my onion jam (page 22), which we sometimes make in the restaurant. If you don't fancy that, the dough itself can be flavoured with a tablespoon chopped fresh herbs, such as thyme or rosemary, or for a more pronounced taste add in up to 4 tablespoons chopped fresh mixed herbs, such as a mixture of flat-leaf parsley, basil and chives, or try adding 4 tablespoons sun-dried tomato pesto (page 228) with 1 teaspoon fennel seeds. Makes 2 loaves

675g (1 ½lb) strong white flour, extra for
  dusting
2 x 7g (¼oz) sachets fast-action dried
  yeast (about 1 tbsp in total)
1 tsp salt
about 450ml (¾ pint) hand-hot water

1 small egg, beaten
1 tbsp milk
100g (4oz) onion jam (page 22)
100g (4oz) Cheddar cheese, grated
butter, to serve

Place the flour in the bowl of a food mixer fitted with a dough attachment if you have one. Add the yeast, salt and the hand-hot water. Switch on the machine and mix until you have a very sloppy dough. Knead on medium speed for a further 6–8 minutes, until you have slightly sticky but pliable dough.

You can also do this by hand: mix the dough with your fingers for 2–3 minutes, then knead to incorporate the flour, scraping the sides of the bowl and folding the dough over itself until it gathers into a rough mass. Turn the dough out onto a well-floured surface and lightly flour your hands. Knead for 6–8 minutes, until the dough is smooth and pliable. The dough will be very sticky at first; keep your hands and the work surface lightly floured, using a dough scraper if necessary to prevent it from sticking and building up on the work surface. As you continue kneading, the dough will become more elastic and easier to handle.

Either way, divide the dough into 2 pieces and knead each one into a long sausage shape about 35cm (14in) long and 5cm (2in) wide. Carefully transfer the loaves to a large non-stick baking sheet, spaced well apart, and slot a piece of parchment paper between them to ensure that they don't stick together. Leave to prove for 1 hour, until doubled in size.

Preheat the oven to 200°C (400°F/gas mark 6).

Mix the egg and milk together in a small bowl, then brush the loaves with the egg wash and bake for 20 minutes. Remove from the oven and then spread over the onion jam and sprinkle the grated cheese on top. Return to the oven and bake for another 20–25 minutes, until the loaves are a deep golden brown and sound hollow when tapped on the bottom. Leave to cool for 5 minutes on the baking sheet, then transfer to a wire rack and leave to cool completely before slicing.

To serve, cut the bread into slices and arrange in a bread basket with a separate pot of butter.

Cherry Tomato, Olive and Rosemary Focaccia

This is one of the breads that we like to serve before the starters arrive in the restaurant. Boilíe goat's cheese also makes a fantastic topping, as it's wonderfully creamy yet has a mild flavour. This is best warm, but it also reheats well or is fine when cold. Makes 1 large flat loaf

450g (1lb) strong white flour, extra for dusting
1 tsp fast-action dried yeast
1 ¼ tsp sea salt flakes
225ml (8fl oz) tepid water
6 tbsp extra virgin olive oil, extra for greasing and drizzling
small handful fresh tiny rosemary sprigs
15 oven-dried cherry tomatoes (page 225)
50g (2oz) pitted black olives, roughly chopped
handful fresh basil leaves

Mix together the flour, yeast and ¼ teaspoon of the salt in a large bowl. Make a well in the centre and pour in the tepid water and 5 tablespoons of the olive oil. Mix well to achieve a soft dough.

Turn the dough out onto a clean surface and knead for 10 minutes, until smooth and elastic. Place in an oiled bowl, cover with oiled clingfilm and leave to rise in a warm place for about 1 hour, until doubled in size.

Turn the dough back out onto a clean surface and knock it back, then knead for another 2–3 minutes and roll out to a large rectangle about 1cm (½in) thick. Place in an oiled, lined baking tin that is 27.5cm x 18cm (11in x 7in) and at least 4cm (1 ½in) deep. Cover with oiled clingfilm. Leave to rise again for 30 minutes.

Meanwhile, preheat the oven to 220°C (425°F/gas mark 7).

Punch holes in the risen dough with your fingers. Stick rosemary sprigs in each hole and scatter over the remaining 1 teaspoon salt. Drizzle with the remaining 1 tablespoon olive oil and bake for about 30 minutes, until risen, cooked through and golden brown. Leave in the tin for a few minutes, then transfer to a wire rack to cool. Arrange the oven-dried cherry tomatoes on top and scatter over the olives and basil leaves, then drizzle with a little olive oil to keep the crust softened.

To serve, transfer the focaccia to a breadboard and cut into chunks, then arrange in a bread basket.

Mediterranean Gluten-free Bread

The number of coeliac customers who come to the restaurant always amazes me. I have my good friend Noleen Boyle, a wonderful pastry chef from Donegal, to thank for this recipe and we always make sure that we have some available for anyone who requests it. Supermarkets are getting much better at stocking gluten-free products, so you should be able to get the tritamyl flour and rice bran from their specialist section. Otherwise, any health food shop should have both. Makes 2 loaves

rapeseed oil, for greasing
100ml (3 ½fl oz) sun-dried tomato pesto (page 228)
6 pitted black olives
small handful fresh basil leaves
500g (1lb 2oz) tritamyl flour (gluten-free flour)
2 tsp gluten-free bread soda
½ tsp salt

325g (11oz) rice bran
150g (5oz) light muscovado sugar
100g (4oz) semolina
750ml (1 ¼ pints) buttermilk
3 eggs
2 tbsp chopped sun-dried tomatoes
1 tbsp sesame seeds
1 tbsp poppy seeds
butter, for spreading

Preheat the oven to 180°C (350°F/gas mark 4). Lightly grease 2 x 1.2 litre (2 pint) loaf tins.

Blitz the sun-dried tomato pesto, olives and basil leaves in a mini blender until fairly smooth.

Sieve the flour into a large bowl with the bread soda and salt, then stir in the rice bran, sugar and semolina. Place the buttermilk, sun-dried tomato pesto mixture, eggs and chopped sun-dried tomatoes in a jug, mixing well to combine.

Make a well in the centre of the flour mixture and pour in the buttermilk mixture, stirring to combine. Spoon the batter into the greased loaf tins and smooth the surface using the back of a spoon. Sprinkle the sesame and poppy seeds on top.

Bake for 1 hour, until the bread is golden brown and crusty on top. Leave in the tin for 5 minutes, then transfer to a wire rack and allow to cool completely.

To serve, place the cooled bread on a breadboard and cut into slices at the table. Hand around a separate pot of butter for spreading.

White Soda Bread

I have a wonderful breakfast chef working with me in the restaurant. Her name is Marie McGloine and every morning she makes this bread for our overnight guests. She's the best baker I've ever seen. We do bake yeast breads too, but this is a traditional Irish white soda bread, which straight out of the oven is hard to beat. Makes 1 loaf

450g (1lb) plain flour, extra for dusting
1 tsp bread soda
1 tsp salt
350ml (12fl oz) buttermilk, extra if necessary
butter, to serve

Preheat the oven to 220°C (425°F/gas mark 7).

Sift the flour, bread soda and salt into a bowl. Make a well in the centre and add the buttermilk. Using a large spoon, mix gently and quickly until you have a nice soft dough. Add a little bit more buttermilk if necessary until the dough binds together without being sloppy.

Knead the dough very lightly on a lightly floured surface and then shape into a round roughly 15cm (6in) in size. Place on a non-stick baking sheet and cut a deep cross in the top.

Bake for 15 minutes, then reduce the oven temperature to 200°C (400°F/gas mark 6) and bake for another 20–25 minutes, or until the loaf is evenly golden and crusty. To check that the bread is properly cooked, tap the base – it should sound hollow. If it doesn't, return it to the oven for another 5 minutes.

Transfer the cooked soda bread to a wire rack and leave to cool for about 20 minutes.

To serve, place the soda bread on a breadboard and cut into slices at the table. Have a dish of butter on hand for spreading. This bread is best eaten while it's still warm.

CHRISTMAS

Roast Turkey with Herb Stuffing

If you want to be sure that your turkey is cooked, invest in a meat thermometer and push it into the thickest part of one of the thighs. This will then clearly show you when the turkey is cooked, leaving no doubt in your mind. Ask your butcher for the giblets with your turkey, as they make excellent stock. I always soak mine in cold water overnight to remove any impurities. Place them in a pan with a chopped carrot and onion, 6 whole peppercorns, 2 bay leaves and a sprig of thyme. Pour in 1.2 litres (2 pints) of water and bring to the boil, then reduce the heat and simmer for 45 minutes. Strain and use as required. **Serves 10–12**

6kg (13lb) oven-ready turkey, at room temperature
  (preferably free range)
100g (4oz) butter, at room temperature
1 tbsp plain flour
3 tbsp ruby red port or red wine
600ml (1 pint) turkey or chicken stock (page 226; see note above)
sea salt and freshly ground black pepper
small bunch of fresh herbs, to garnish (to include rosemary,
  sage and thyme)
crispy roast potatoes (page 152), to serve
roasted root vegetables with sesame seeds (page 156), to serve
Brussels sprout crumble (page 159), to serve

Herb stuffing:
75g (3oz) butter
1 large onion, diced
175g (6oz) fresh white breadcrumbs
1 tbsp chopped fresh flat-leaf parsley
1 tsp chopped fresh sage
1 tsp chopped fresh thyme leaves

Preheat the oven to 190°C (375°F/gas mark 5).

To make the stuffing, melt the butter in a frying pan over a medium heat. Add the onion and cook for a few minutes, until softened but not coloured. Place the breadcrumbs in a bowl and tip in the cooked onion and the parsley, sage and thyme. Mix well to combine and season to taste.

To stuff the turkey, start at the neck end, where you'll find a flap of loose skin. Gently loosen this away from the breast and you'll be able to make a triangular pocket. Pack the stuffing inside as far as you can go and make a neat round shape on the outside, then tuck the neck flap under the turkey and secure it with a small skewer.

Smear the skin of the turkey all over with most of the butter and season generously. Turn the turkey breast side up and tie the tops of the drumsticks with string. Weigh the turkey to calculate the required cooking time, allowing 20 minutes per 450g (1lb) plus 20 minutes extra – a 6kg (13lb) turkey should take about 4 hours 40 minutes to cook.

Lay a large sheet of foil lengthways over a large roasting tin, leaving enough at each end to wrap over the turkey, then lightly butter the foil. Repeat this with another sheet of foil, this time across the tin. Lightly butter the foil once again. Place the stuffed turkey breast side up in the centre of the foil, then wrap loosely to enclose, allowing air to circulate around the turkey.

Place in the oven and cook according to your calculated cooking time, carefully unwrapping and basting every 40 minutes. For the final hour, fold back the foil and use it to cover the ends of the drumsticks to prevent them from burning. Baste well and return to the oven. The turkey should be a rich, dark brown colour. To be sure it's cooked, insert a fine skewer into the thickest part of the thigh: the juices should run clear, but if they are still pink, return the turkey to the oven and check again every 15 minutes until you are happy that the turkey is cooked right the way through. Remove from the oven and transfer to a warmed serving platter. Cover with foil and leave to rest in a warm place for at least 10 minutes, or up to 30 minutes is fine.

Remove the foil from the roasting tin and pour any juices that collected in it into the tin. Place the tin directly on the hob over a gentle heat and skim off any excess fat from the cooking juices. Stir the flour into the tin's residue. Cook on the hob for 1–2 minutes, stirring until golden. Pour in the port or red wine, stirring to combine, then gradually add the stock, stirring until smooth after each addition. Bring to the boil and let it bubble for about 10 minutes, until reduced and thickened to a gravy consistency, stirring occasionally. Season to taste.

To serve, garnish the turkey with the bunch of herbs in the cavity and bring to the table. Carve into slices and arrange on warmed serving plates with some of the gravy, the roast potatoes, roasted root vegetables and Brussels sprout crumble.

Maple Glazed Ham with Pineapple Salsa

A traditional ham is the perfect choice if you've got hordes of visitors to feed, so it's especially good to have over the festive period. A certain crowd pleaser, it tastes equally good served hot or cold. Have you ever wondered what the difference is between ham, bacon and gammon? Bacon is cured pork; gammon is a hind leg cut of bacon; and once gammon is cooked, it's called ham. Any leftovers from this ham or a turkey can be used in countless other dishes, such as in a creamy filling for vol-au-vents, in risottos or just the ham is excellent for a spaghetti carbonara, so there's no waste – even the bone will make a wonderful stock. **Serves 10–12**

5.25kg (11lb) leg of gammon (on the bone and skin on)
4 celery sticks, roughly chopped
2 onions, sliced
1 bunch of fresh thyme
1 tbsp black peppercorns
200ml (7fl oz) Irish whiskey
200ml (7fl oz) maple syrup
2 tbsp redcurrant jelly
2 tbsp balsamic vinegar
1 tbsp ground allspice
1 tbsp whole cloves

Pineapple salsa:
1 ripe pineapple, peeled, cored and cut into 1cm (½in) dice
1 tbsp caster sugar
1 small red onion, finely chopped
finely grated rind and juice of 1 lime
½ large red chilli, seeded and finely chopped
1 tbsp chopped fresh mint
1 tbsp chopped fresh coriander
2 tsp freshly grated root ginger
sea salt and freshly ground black pepper

Although gammon is less salty nowadays, soaking is still a good idea. Place the gammon in a large pan and cover with cold water. Leave to soak for at least 6 hours or overnight is best, then drain.

Weigh the gammon joint and calculate the cooking time, allowing 20 minutes per 450g (1lb) plus 20 minutes – a 5.25kg (11lb) joint should take about 4 hours. Place in a large pan, cover with water and bring to the boil, skimming off any scum. Add the celery, onions, thyme and peppercorns and return to the boil, then cover, reduce the heat and simmer until completely tender, occasionally skimming off any scum that rises to the top. If you aren't sure the gammon is properly cooked, check the bone end – it should come away freely from the gammon joint. Drain and leave until it's cool enough to handle.

Preheat the oven to 180°C (350°F/gas mark 4).

Carefully peel away the skin, leaving the layer of white fat intact. Using a sharp knife, score the fat diagonally to make a diamond pattern, being careful not to cut into the meat. Place the whiskey in a pan with the maple syrup, redcurrant jelly, balsamic vinegar and ground allspice. Bring to the boil and simmer for about 10 minutes, until slightly thickened. Stud the ham with the cloves and place in a large roasting tin with a little water to prevent the bottom from catching and burning. Brush a layer of the syrup all over the ham, reserving the remainder. Cook for 1 hour, brushing over another layer of the glaze every 15 minutes, until it's all gone. Remove the cooked ham from the oven, transfer to a serving platter and leave to rest for 15 minutes.

Meanwhile, make the pineapple salsa. Mix the diced pineapple with the sugar. Heat a non-stick frying pan over a high heat, add the pineapple and cook quickly for about 2 minutes to lightly caramelise it. Tip into a bowl and add the onion, lime rind and juice, chilli, herbs and ginger. Season to taste and set aside to allow the flavours to develop.

To serve, carve slices from one side of the ham, cutting diagonally to achieve an even thickness. When you reach the bone, insert the knife at a flatter angle and slice across the top of the bone. Turn over the leg to carve slices from the other sides. Arrange on serving plates with spoonfuls of the pineapple salsa.

Turkey Satay Vegetable Noodles

This recipe is great to use up any leftover turkey from Christmas Day. It packs a powerful flavour punch and is just the ticket after the excesses of the festive season. Stir-frying is a traditional Chinese cooking technique that's very easy to master. To check if the vegetables are cooked, pierce them with the tip of a knife – they should feel as soft as butter. Serves 4–6

275g (10oz) fine egg noodles
1 tbsp sunflower oil
1 large red pepper, halved, seeded and thinly sliced
225g (8oz) fine green beans, trimmed and halved
175g (6oz) baby corn, halved lengthways
2 garlic cloves, crushed
400g (14oz) can coconut milk
350g (12oz) leftover cooked turkey meat, cut into bite-sized pieces
100g (4oz) crunchy peanut butter
2 tbsp dark soy sauce
2 tbsp sweet chilli sauce
1 tsp light muscovado sugar
juice of ½ lime
50g (2oz) cashew nuts, toasted and finely chopped
handful fresh coriander leaves, to garnish

Place the fine egg noodles in a pan of boiling water and cook for 3–4 minutes, until tender, or according to the packet instructions.

Heat a wok until very hot. Add the oil and swirl it around the edges, then tip in the red pepper, green beans, baby corn and garlic and stir-fry for 3–4 minutes, until the vegetables are tender, sprinkling over 1 tablespoon of water if the mixture is getting too dry.

Drain the noodles and add to the wok with the coconut milk, turkey, peanut butter, soy sauce, chilli sauce, sugar and lime juice. Stir-fry for another 2–3 minutes, until all the ingredients are piping hot.

To serve, divide among warmed serving bowls and scatter over the cashew nuts and coriander.

Auntie Maureen's Plum Pudding

Nothing beats the flavour of homemade Christmas pudding. I love it hot or cold, with lashings of cream, but the brandy and rum crème analgaise is even more special. I always look forward to it. A big thank you to Auntie Maureen for sharing her recipe. **Makes 2 x 1.2 litre (2 pint) puddings**

50g (2oz) plain flour
½ tsp ground mixed spice
½ tsp ground cloves
¼ tsp ground nutmeg
225g (8oz) sultanas
175g (6oz) fresh white breadcrumbs
175g (6oz) butter, melted, extra for
  greasing
175g (6oz) light muscovado sugar
175g (6oz) raisins
50g (2oz) currants
50g (2oz) candied mixed peel

50g (2oz) blanched almonds, chopped
½ apple, peeled, cored and diced
½ small carrot, grated
finely grated rind and juice of 1 lemon
2 eggs, lightly beaten
300ml (½ pint) stout
fresh redcurrant sprigs, to decorate
  (optional)
icing sugar, for dusting (optional)
brandy and rum crème anglaise
  (page 231), to serve

Sift together the flour, mixed spice, cloves and nutmeg. Add the sultanas, breadcrumbs, melted butter, sugar, raisins, currants, mixed peel, almonds, apple, carrot and the lemon rind and juice and mix until well combined. Gradually add the beaten eggs, stirring constantly, followed by the stout. Mix everything thoroughly and cover with a clean tea towel, then leave in a cool place overnight.

Grease 2 x 1.2 litre (2 pint) pudding bowls and fill with the fruit mixture. Cover with a double thickness of greaseproof paper and tin foil, then tie tightly under the rim with string. Store in a cool, dry place for up to 4 months.

To cook, preheat the oven to 150°C (300°F/gas mark 2) and stand each pudding basin in a large cake tin three-quarters full of boiling water. Cook for 6–8 hours (or you can steam them for 6 hours in the usual way). Allow the puddings to cool, then re-cover with clean greaseproof paper. Again, store in a cool, dry place.

On Christmas Day, re-cover with new greaseproof paper and foil. Steam for 2–3 hours, until completely cooked through and tender. Decorate with redcurrant sprigs and a light dusting of icing sugar, if liked.

To serve, cut the plum pudding into slices and arrange on serving plates. Have a separate jug of the brandy and rum crème anglaise so that everyone can help themselves.

MacNean Old-fashioned Mincemeat Pies

Not surprisingly, my Auntie Maureen is also the champion of this Maguire classic. Before she retired, she was a Domestic Science teacher in Cavan, and I don't believe she ever had a pupil who didn't learn how to make her marvellous mincemeat pies. Once you've made it yourself, you'll never buy another jar of the stuff again. Why not make twice the amount of mincemeat and put it into some sterilised fancy jars, wrap with a red ribbon and give a jar to your friends for a Christmas gift? **Makes 12**

Sweet pastry:
175g (6oz) plain flour
100g (4oz) butter
50g (2oz) caster sugar
pinch of salt
1 egg yolk
½ tbsp cream
½ tsp fresh lemon juice
1 egg, beaten

Mincemeat:
50g (2oz) eating apple, peeled, cored and finely chopped
25g (1oz) butter, melted
25g (1oz) raisins
25g (1oz) sultanas
25g (1oz) currants
2 tbsp Irish whiskey
1 tbsp candied citrus peel
2 tsp finely chopped blanched almonds
2 tsp dark muscovado sugar
finely grated rind of ½ small orange
finely grated rind of ½ lemon
good pinch of ground nutmeg
good pinch of ground cinnamon
good pinch of ground cloves
pinch of salt
icing sugar, to dust

To make the mincemeat, mix all the ingredients together in a large bowl (except the icing sugar) and cover with a clean tea towel. Leave for 2 days in a cool, dark place for the flavours to develop, then pack into clean, dry jars. Seal and store in a cool, dark place for 3 weeks before using.

To make the pastry, place the flour, butter, sugar and salt into a food processor and blend for 20 seconds. Add the egg yolk, cream and lemon juice and blend again until the pastry comes together. Do not overwork or the pastry will be tough. Wrap in clingfilm and chill for 1 hour.

Preheat the oven to 180°C (350°F/gas mark 4).

Roll out half of the pastry thinly on a lightly floured board. Cut out 12 x 7cm (3in) rounds with a cutter and use to line the bottom of a bun tin, then fill with the mincemeat.

Roll out the rest of the pastry and cut 12 x 6cm (2 ½in) rounds with a cutter to fit the tops. Brush the edges with water and place the rounds on top of the filled pies in the tin, sealing with the tips of your fingers. Make a small slit in each mince pie and brush with the beaten egg. Bake for 15–16 minutes, until cooked through and golden brown. Cool in the tins before lifting out the mince pies.

To serve, dust the mince pies with icing sugar and arrange on a large serving platter.

Wilted Spinach

Serves 6

100g (4oz) butter
550g (1lb 4oz) spinach, tough stalks
  removed
pinch of caster sugar
sea salt and freshly ground black pepper

Heat a pan over a medium heat and add the butter. Once it has stopped foaming, quickly sauté the spinach with the sugar until soft and wilted. Season to taste and drain well on kitchen paper to remove the excess moisture. Return to the pan and keep warm. Use as required.

Oven-dried Cherry Tomatoes

Makes 20

10 cherry tomatoes, halved
4 tbsp olive oil
good pinch chopped fresh thyme
sea salt and freshly ground black pepper

Preheat the oven to 100°C (200°F/gas mark ¼).

Arrange the cherry tomato halves cut side up on a baking sheet lined with parchment paper. Drizzle over the olive oil, scatter the thyme on top and season to taste. Place in the middle of the oven for 4–5 hours, checking every hour to ensure the tomatoes at the edge of the sheet aren't overcooking. Remove the tomatoes from the oven and leave to cool, then use as required. These tomatoes can be kept covered with olive oil in a sterilised jar in the fridge for up to 2 weeks. Drain and bring back to room temperature to use.

Vegetable Stock

Makes about 1.2 litres (2 pints)

2 leeks, trimmed and finely chopped
2 onions, finely chopped
2 carrots, finely chopped
2 celery sticks, finely chopped
1 fennel bulb, finely chopped
1 garlic bulb, sliced in half crossways
1 fresh thyme sprig
1 bay leaf
1 star anise
100ml (3 ½fl oz) dry white wine
1 tsp pink peppercorns
1 tsp coriander seeds
pinch of salt

Place all the ingredients in a large pan and cover with 1.75 litres (3 pints) cold water. Cover with a lid and bring to a simmer, then remove the lid and cook for 30 minutes, until the vegetables are tender.

Either set aside to marinate for 2 days in a cool place, or if you're short of time, strain through a sieve. Taste – if you find the flavour isn't full enough, return to the pan and reduce until you're happy with it. Leave to cool completely and then transfer to a plastic jug with a lid and store in the fridge until needed. Use as required. This will keep in the fridge for up to 3 days or freeze in 600ml (1 pint) cartons and defrost when you need it.

Chicken Stock

Makes about 1.2 litres (2 pints)

1 large raw or cooked chicken carcass,
    skin and fat removed and bones
    chopped
2 leeks, trimmed and chopped
2 onions, chopped
2 carrots, chopped
2 celery sticks, chopped
1 fresh thyme sprig
1 bay leaf
handful of fresh parsley stalks
1 tsp white peppercorns

If using a raw chicken carcass, preheat the oven to 220°C (450°F/gas mark 7) and roast the chicken carcass in a tin for about 40 minutes, until golden. Drain through a colander to get rid of excess fat, then chop it up.

Place the chopped-up chicken carcass in a large pan and cover with 1.8 litres (3 ¼ pints) cold water. Bring to the boil, then skim off any fat and scum from the surface. Reduce the heat to a simmer and tip in all the remaining ingredients.

Simmer gently for another 1–1 ½ hours, skim-ming occasionally and topping up with water as necessary. Taste regularly to check the flavour. When you're happy with it, remove from the heat and pass through a sieve. Leave to cool and remove any fat that settles on the top, then store in the fridge in a plastic jug with a lid and use as required. This can be stored in the fridge for up to 3 days or freeze in 600ml (1 pint) cartons and defrost when you need it.

Fish Stock

Makes about 2 litres (3½ pints)

250g (9oz) white fish trimmings and/or
    bones (such as lemon sole, brill or plaice
    bones)
3 leeks, trimmed and chopped
3 carrots, chopped
1 fennel bulb, chopped
large handful of fresh parsley, roughly
    chopped
175ml (6fl oz) dry white wine

Rinse the fish bones and trimmings of any blood, which would make the stock look cloudy and taste bitter. Place into a large pan with the leeks, carrots, fennel and parsley. Pour in the white wine, then add 2.4 litres (4 pints) cold water to cover the fish and vegetables. Place on a high heat and bring to a simmer. After 5 minutes, remove the scum that forms on the surface with a spoon and discard. Reduce the heat and simmer, covered, for about 25 minutes, skimming as necessary.

At the end of the cooking time, remove the stock from the heat and strain, discarding the fish trimmings and the vegetables. Cool and store in a plastic covered jug in the fridge and use as required. This can be stored in the fridge for up to 3 days. Alternatively, once the stock is made you can reduce it further and then freeze it in ice cube trays (freezing it this way means you can defrost as little or as much as you need at a time).

Beef Stock

Makes about 1.75 litres (3 pints)

675g (1 ½lb) shin of beef, cut into pieces
675g (1 ½lb) marrow bones or knuckle of
  veal, chopped
1 tbsp olive oil
1 onion, sliced
1 carrot, sliced
1 celery stick, sliced
1 tbsp tomato purée
150ml (¼ pint) red wine
1 small garlic bulb, halved
1 bouquet garni (parsley stalks, sprigs of
  thyme and bay leaf tied together)

Preheat the oven to 220°C (425°F/gas
mark 7).

Place the shin of beef and marrow bones or
knuckle of veal in a roasting tin and cook in the
oven for 30–40 minutes, until well browned.
Drain off all the excess oil and discard.

Meanwhile, heat the olive oil in a large pan
over a medium heat. Add the onion, carrot
and celery and sauté for 6–7 minutes, until
just beginning to colour. Stir in the tomato
purée, then pour in the red wine and allow it
to bubble down for 1 minute.

Add the roasted meat bones to the vegetables
and wine along with the garlic and bouquet
garni. Pour in 1.75 litres (3 pints) water and
bring to the boil. Skim off any scum, then
partially cover and reduce the heat to simmer
for 4–5 hours, until you have achieved a well-
flavoured stock, topping up occasionally with
a little water. You'll need to add another 1.2
litres (2 pints) in total over the whole cooking
time.

Strain the stock and leave to cool completely
before chilling down. Once it's cold, remove

any trace of solidified fat from the surface
using a large spoon, then cover with a lid
and return to the fridge until needed. Use as
required. This stores very well in the fridge for
3 days or freeze in 600ml (1 pint) cartons and
defrost when you need it.

Variation

Lamb Stock
Use lamb bones instead of the beef.

Basil Pesto

Makes about 250ml (9fl oz)

1 large bunch of fresh basil leaves (at
  least 50g (2oz))
2 garlic cloves, peeled
25g (1oz) pine nuts, toasted
175ml (6fl oz) olive or rapeseed oil
50g (2oz) freshly grated Parmesan
sea salt and freshly ground black pepper

Place the basil in a food processor with the
garlic, pine nuts and a quarter of the oil. Blend
to a paste, then slowly add the remaining oil
through the feeder tube. Transfer to a bowl
and fold in the Parmesan, then season to taste.
Cover with clingfilm and chill until needed.
This will keep happily in the fridge for up to 1
week – just top it up with a little extra olive oil
to keep it tasting lovely and fresh. It can also
be frozen. Use as required.

Sun-dried Tomato Pesto

Makes about 400ml (14fl oz)

175g (6oz) semi-sun-dried tomatoes,
  roughly chopped
8 large fresh basil leaves
2 garlic cloves, peeled
200ml (7fl oz) olive or rapeseed oil
sea salt and freshly ground black pepper

Place the semi-sun-dried tomatoes in a food
processor or blender with the basil leaves and
garlic and pulse to finely chop. Switch the
machine back on and slowly pour in the oil
through the feeder tube until the pesto has
emulsified. Transfer to a bowl with a spatula
and season to taste. This can be made up to
3–4 days in advance and kept covered with
clingfilm in the fridge. Use as required.

Honey and Clove Sauce

Makes about 200ml (7fl oz)

225ml (8fl oz) beef stock (page 227)
4 tbsp clear honey
2 tbsp light muscovado sugar
2 tbsp dark soy sauce
2 tbsp balsamic vinegar
2 tbsp tomato ketchup
2 tsp whole cloves
sea salt and freshly ground black pepper

Place the stock, honey, sugar, soy sauce, vinegar, ketchup and cloves in a small pan. Bring to the boil, then reduce the heat and simmer vigorously for 5 minutes, until the mixture has thickened to a sauce consistency that coats the back of a spoon. Season to taste, then pass through a sieve into a clean pan, discarding the cloves. Reheat gently and use as required. This will keep for up to 1 week in the fridge in a rigid plastic container. It can also be frozen. Use as required.

Variation

Honey and Ginger Sauce
Use a 5cm (2in) piece of peeled and sliced root ginger instead of the cloves.

Balsamic Syrup

Makes about 120ml (4fl oz)

100g (4oz) caster sugar
100ml (3 ½fl oz) ruby red port
100ml (3 ½fl oz) balsamic vinegar

Place the sugar, port and balsamic vinegar in a heavy-based pan. Bring to the boil, then reduce the heat and simmer for 15–20 minutes, until the mixture has reduced by one-third and has become thick and syrupy, like a honey consistency. Serve at once or allow to cool completely and store in a bowl covered with clingfilm in the fridge for up to 1 month. When you're ready to use it, if you find that it has solidified too much, either warm it in a small pan or in the microwave. Or if you want to use it cold, add a few drops of boiling water to it, stirring to loosen. Use as required.

Balsamic Cream

Vary the type of stock you use depending on what you are serving with this.

Makes 150ml (¼ pint)

150ml (¼ pint) beef stock (page 227) or
  chicken stock (page 226)
150ml (¼ pint) cream
2 tbsp balsamic vinegar
1 tbsp tomato purée
sea salt and freshly ground black pepper

Place the stock, cream, vinegar and tomato purée in a small pan. Bring to the boil, then reduce the heat and simmer for 20–25 minutes, until reduced by a quarter and thickened to a sauce consistency. Season to taste. Use immediately or leave to cool, then transfer to a bowl and cover with clingfilm and chill until required.

Red Wine Sauce

Makes 200ml (7fl oz)

300ml (½ pint) red wine
2 tbsp balsamic vinegar
200ml (7fl oz) beef stock (page 227)
2 tbsp chopped fresh thyme
2 heaped tsp light muscovado sugar
sea salt and freshly ground black pepper

Heat a small pan and pour in the red wine and vinegar. Boil for about 5 minutes, until reduced by half. Add the stock, thyme and sugar and reduce again for another 10–12 minutes, stirring occasionally, until you have achieved a good sauce consistency. Season to taste and use as required. This will keep for up to 1 week in the fridge in a rigid plastic container. It can also be frozen. Use as required.

Variation

Madeira Sauce
Replace the red wine with Madeira.

Crème Anglaise

Makes about 400ml (14fl oz)

5 egg yolks
3 tbsp caster sugar
½ vanilla pod, split in half and seeds
    scraped out
300ml (½ pint) milk
100ml (3 ½fl oz) cream

Place the egg yolks in a large bowl with the sugar and vanilla seeds. Whisk with an electric mixer for a few minutes, until pale and thickened.

Place the milk and cream in a medium pan and bring to the boil, then immediately remove from the heat.

Gradually whisk the heated milk and cream into the egg yolk mixture until smooth, then pour back into the pan and place over a gentle heat. Cook gently for 6–8 minutes on a medium heat, stirring constantly, until the custard coats the back of a wooden spoon. Serve hot or transfer to a large bowl. Press a sheet of clingfilm directly onto the surface of the custard to help prevent a skin forming and leave to cool, then chill until needed. It can also be put into a squeezy bottle, depending on how you want to use it. Use warm or cold, as required. This will keep in the fridge for 2–3 days.

Variation

Brandy and Rum Crème Anglaise
Add 2 tablespoons of brandy and 2 tablespoons of dark rum to the crème anglaise before it gets cooked to thicken.

White Chocolate Curls

Makes 10–15

100g good-quality bar of white chocolate

Using a large-bladed knife held with both hands or a cheese slice, pull the blade across the chocolate, pressing down slightly. As the blade comes towards you, the chocolate will form curls (if the chocolate is too hard, it will be brittle and will break rather than forming curls, in which case leave it at room temperature for 5 minutes before trying again). You will find that as the chocolate bar gets thinner it will be harder to form nice curls. These can be made up to 24 hours in advance and carefully layered up in pieces of parchment paper in a large airtight container. Keep in the fridge and just be careful that none of the curls are touching each other or they may get damaged. Use as required.

Index